Grammar Choices for Graduate and Professional Writers

Nigel A. Caplan

Ann Arbor
University of Michigan Press

ISBN-13: 978-0-472-03501-4

2015   2014   2013   2012   4   3   2   1

Acknowledgments

This book has existed in numerous versions, and I owe my thanks to everyone who was subjected to early forms of these materials: to the students and postdocs at the University of North Carolina at Chapel Hill who kept asking me difficult grammar questions; to my students and colleagues at the University of Delaware, who have unwittingly piloted the book; to Dr. Scott Stevens, director of the UD English Language Institute, for giving me release time to complete what did not turn out to be the final draft of the manuscript; and to Chris Feak for blazing the trail and generously guiding me on each successive draft. This project would never have come to fruition without the encouragement and expertise of Kelly Sippell at the University of Michigan Press, graduate education's number one supporter. Finally, I could not write without the patience of my family tolerating my periodic absences; thank you, Ellisha and Sam, and thank you in advance to Aidan, born as this book went to press. I would like to dedicate *Grammar Choices* to my parents, who first instilled in me the importance of choosing the right words.

Nigel A. Caplan
University of Delaware English Language Institute

Grateful acknowledgment is made to the following authors, publishers, and journals for permission to reprint previously published materials.

Mark Davies for material from the Corpus of Contemporary American English.

Emerald Group Publishing for material from *Disaster Prevention Management:* Pilot assessment of an experiential disaster communication curriculum by D.B. Friedman, I.D. Rose, and A. Koskan, *20,* 238–250.

The University of Michigan for material from the Michigan Corpus of Upper-level Student Papers (MICUSP).

Every effort has been made to contact the copyright holders for permission to reprint borrowed material. We regret any oversights that may have occurred and will rectify them in future printings of this book.

Contents

Introduction

Every sentence you write for a university assignment, master's thesis, doctoral dissertation, or research paper is the result of many choices: past or present tense? active or passive voice? *I* or *the author*? coordination or subordination? *the* study or *a* study? Grammar is the system of choices that create meaning in a language. You might not think about all these choices all the time, but as a reader, you are influenced by the effects of these language choices. *Grammar Choices* is a guide to the choices available to you as an academic writer in English. Although there are certainly some *rules* governing acceptable and unacceptable grammar, there are far more *choices* to be made among grammatically acceptable forms that have different meanings. If you can control these meanings, you will communicate more effectively and efficiently in your graduate-level and professional academic writing.

Grammar Choices is a different kind of grammar book:

- It is written for graduate students, including master's, MBA, and doctoral candidates, as well as postdoctoral researchers and faculty.[1]

- It describes the language of advanced academic writing with more than 300 real examples from successful graduate students and from published texts.

- Grammar is presented through a functional description of the resources used to create meaning clearly, communicate with the reader appropriately, and organize a message effectively (Halliday, 1994, p. xiii).

- Dozens of exercises provide practice in understanding, analyzing, and most importantly, using the grammar in practical written contexts.

- Examples and exercises are drawn from corpora,[2] published research, and student samples.

- Vocabulary building is integrated in the grammar presentations and practice activities; the companion website offers vocabulary lists and quizzes.

- Students are encouraged to investigate the language choices that are typical of their own academic disciplines or professional fields through structured reading and writing activities.

- The last two units go beyond the scope of traditional grammar books: Unit 7 teaches how to use corpora to find and use collocations, and Unit 8 presents the grammatical resources used to organize information beyond the sentence level.

- *Grammar Choices* is cross-referenced with *Academic Writing for Graduate Students*, 3rd edition (Swales & Feak, 2012) and sometimes with the volumes in the *English for Today's Research World* series (Feak & Swales, 2009, 2011; Swales & Feak, 2009, 2011).

---

[1] Throughout the book, I use the North American terminology of *undergraduate* (bachelor's) degrees and *graduate* (master's and doctoral) degrees. In other countries, graduate students are called post-graduates. MBA stands for Masters of Business Administration.

[2] A corpus (plural: *corpora*) is a large collection of digital texts that can be considered representative of a particular type of language. *Grammar Choices* primarily draws from two online corpora: the *Michigan Corpus of Upper-level Student Papers* (MICUSP), which reveals many of the choices that successful graduate students make in their writing, and the *Corpus of Contemporary American English* (COCA), which collects published academic writing and allows for comparisons between it and spoken English, journalism, and fiction.

Grammar Choices does not attempt to cover all the possible grammar choices in English—that would be a much longer book! The selection of structures is deliberately limited to those that are most useful to graduate and research writers, according to analyses of actual academic writing. Important differences from other forms of writing and spoken English are noted where they might help prevent ineffective choices. Although there are certainly differences in language use between fields (disciplines) and genres (text types), the grammar and vocabulary targeted in *Grammar Choices* will help you be more aware of academic language as you read and are more deliberate in your choices as you write.

Grammar Choices can be used as a stand-alone textbook, for self-study, or as a companion to *Academic Writing for Graduate Students*, 3rd edition (Swales and Feak, 2012) or the volumes in the *English in Today's Research World* series (also by Swales and Feak), all published by the University of Michigan Press (www.press.umich.edu/esl/compsite/ETRW/).

Unit Walk-Through

Each of the eight units in *Grammar Choices* contains:

1. an **overview** of the grammar topic
2. a **preview** test that allows students to assess their control of the target grammar and instructors to diagnose areas of difficulty
3. an **authentic example** of graduate student writing showing the unit grammar in use
4. **clear descriptions** of essential grammar structures using the framework of functional grammar, cutting-edge research in applied linguistics, and corpus studies
5. **authentic examples** for every grammar point from corpora and published texts (including original in-text citations)
6. **vocabulary** relevant to the grammar point—for example, common verbs in the passive voice, summary nouns used with *this/these*, and irregular plural nouns
7. **exercises** for every grammar point to help writers develop grammatical awareness and use grammar effectively, including completing sentences, writing, revising, paraphrasing, and editing; most exercises use authentic items from the *Michigan Corpus of Upper-level Student Papers* (MICUSP) or the *Corpus of Contemporary American English* (COCA); published books, articles, and websites; or samples of strong graduate-student writing
8. **grammar in your discipline**, a section inviting writers to investigate discipline-specific language use and apply it to an academic genre.

Vocabulary

Vocabulary lists for each unit are available for teachers online. Words have been selected if they are:

- from the Academic Word List, or AWL (Coxhead, 2000), a useful list of 560 word families that are commonly found in academic writing across disciplines; more than

300 of the AWL word families[3] are targeted in *Grammar Choices*, and many more are used incidentally.

- beyond the first 2,000 word families of English, according to the British National Corpus;[4] everyday language has consistently been found to rely on a vocabulary of about 2,000 word families, so less frequent words are likely to be typical of advanced academic and technical writing (Hinkel, 2004, p. 99).

- the vocabulary of research and graduate study, such as *methodology* and *statistically significant.*

- collocations (words that frequently occur together) and other chunks of vocabulary that are idiomatic in academic writing.

- interesting and useful words that will expand the writer's choices and sophistication.

Grammar Terminology

Every grammar book needs a **metalanguage**, words to describe the grammar. Although most of the terms used in *Grammar Choices* should be familiar, some need a word of explanation.

- Clauses are described as **finite** or **non-finite** (Unit 1). A finite clause contains at least a subject and a finite verb. Non-finite clauses include all *–ing* clauses and *to* infinitive clauses as well as reduced relative clauses (for example, *the article published in Science*), which are called adjective phrases in some grammar books. It is important to use the term *non-finite clause* because it helps explain the structure of *–ing* and *to* infinitive clauses: like their finite counterparts, non-finite verbs can be transitive or intransitive. For example, *using* is transitive and requires an example. Therefore, *using a computer* is grammatical, but just *using* is not.

- The elements of a clause that are controlled by the verb are called its **complements** (Unit 1). Complements include direct objects, indirect objects, noun clauses, and non-finite clauses. A key distinction is that a complement cannot usually change its position in a clause, unlike an adverbial (a prepositional phrase or adverb). For example, it would be unusual to write *In the glass water remained* instead of *Water remained in the glass* because *in the glass* is a complement of the verb *remain*. However, both *In the morning, the glass was empty* and *The glass was empty in the morning* are acceptable because *in the morning* is a prepositional phrase that expresses time and modifies the whole clause.

- In describing clause combination, I have distinguished between two different techniques: Unit 2 teaches patterns for combining clauses into longer sentences, which I have called **equal clauses** (compound sentences) and **unequal clauses** (independent clause plus one or more dependent clauses). Unit 3 teaches clauses that are **embedded** inside a main clause: restrictive relative clauses (which become part of a noun phrase) and noun clauses (which function as the complement of a verb, noun, or adjective). I

---

[3] In vocabulary analysis, a word family includes all related items, so *analysis, analyze, analytic,* and *analyst* are four words from one family.

[4] These lists are generated using Tom Cobb's invaluable *Complete Lexical Tutor* (www.lextutor.ca).

have generally avoided the term **complex sentence** since it covers sentences with all types of subordinate clauses (adverb clauses, restrictive and non-restrictive relative clauses, and noun clauses) and hides the important difference in structure and meaning between unequal clauses and embedded clauses.

- There is little agreement on the naming of **verb tenses**. *Grammar Choices* uses the convention *time + aspect*, for example, present simple, present perfect, and past simple (Unit 4). This produces a completely regular system, which should be clearer for learners. In some grammar books, all tenses follow this convention except simple ones (*present perfect* but *simple present*), which seems unnecessarily confusing.

Since *Grammar Choices* includes only the grammar relevant for academic written English, instructors looking for a description of structures that are beyond the scope of this book should refer to Keith S. Folse's *Keys to Teaching Grammar to English Language Learners: A Practical Handbook* (University of Michigan Press, 2009).

This textbook is based on the description of language known as systemic functional linguistics, or functional grammar (Halliday, 1994). Functional grammar describes how speakers and writers make choices within grammatical systems to control meaning at three levels: experiential, interpersonal, and textual (1.8). The first five units are mostly concerned with the experiential level (What happened?). Unit 6 focuses on ways to create interpersonal meaning with evaluative language (What is the relationship between the reader and writer?), and Unit 8 teaches paragraph structure through the textual function of grammar (How is the message organized through the text?).

Functional grammar was chosen because it illuminates how choices between equally "correct" alternatives are rarely arbitrary or insignificant. For example, the choice of passive over active voice might hide the agent of the verb (changing the experiential and interpersonal meanings) or move old information into the subject position, thus better highlighting new information (changing the textual meaning). Verb tenses also demonstrate this effect: *the results were influential* and *the results have been influential* describe the same experience with the same textual organization, but they vary in *interpersonal meaning*: the present perfect makes the results still influential today, while the past simple suggests that the writer no longer sees the results as so influential.

One obstacle for newcomers to functional grammar is its metalanguage, which is very different from the structural grammar that is better known to many instructors and students. For example, in functional grammar a clause is described in terms of its participants (subjects and complements), processes (verbs), and adjuncts (prepositional phrases and adverbs). This can create a regrettable barrier to seeing the profound implications of functional grammar. Consequently, I have chosen to use a more familiar metalanguage while still retaining a focus on the use—rather than the "rules"—of grammar. Excellent introductions to systemic functional linguistics can be found in Eggins (2004) and Lock (1995). I hope that readers see the value of a functional approach to grammar, while functional grammarians excuse the liberties I have taken to make this powerful system of grammar accessible and useful for graduate and professional writers.

An Approach to Academic Written Grammar

This unit describes the building blocks of written grammar: word forms, phrases, and clauses. Unit 1 provides a way of talking about grammar (a metalanguage) and introduces three important ideas:

- Writing can be broken into "slots." A sentence is comprised of clauses, and each clause has slots for a subject, verb, and usually a complement or two. Only certain word forms can fill those slots.

- Grammar is more than a set of rules for what you *must* write; it is a range of choices for what you *can* write.

- Your choices create three levels of meaning at the same time—the content of your sentence, your attitude or relationship with the reader, and the organization of the text.

Michael Halliday, whose functional description of grammar underlies these principles wrote: "everything has to be described before everything else" (Halliday & Matthiessen, 2004, p. 62); therefore, you will see many cross-references to other parts of this textbook, and you may refer to this unit when you are studying a later section. In this book, a cross reference in this format (2.5) means you should refer to Unit 2, Section 5.

UNIT 1 Preview Test

These sentences are not grammatical in written academic English. Find the errors and correct them.

1. This failure was occurred for two reasons.

2. Intensity is a significant in stress production.

3. He indicated me that he had decided to always choose the second syllable.

4. I do not agree that conclusion.

5. This experiment focuses the role of pitch.

6. We would suggest to find a better connector piece.

7. This would have allowed to test spheres.

8. After reviewing customer specifications, five main design concepts generated.

9. We talked Terry Larrow.

10. $1500 cost our prototype.

Grammar Awareness: Report

Read the excerpt from a report written by a student in a psychology course included in the Michigan Corpus of Upper-level Student Papers (MICUSP). Like all the writing in MICUSP, it received an A grade. Then complete the tasks on page 3.

1 Researchers have previously <u>studied</u> and <u>suggested</u> interventions <u>designed</u> to increase women in math and science and change the environment and attitudes. Steele (1997) <u>implemented</u> a program called "wise" schooling, Nauta et al. (1998) suggested interventions designed to increase self-efficacy in math and science, and Gavin and Reis (2003) <u>proposed</u> guidelines for teachers in the classroom.

2 Steele's (1997) "wise" schooling was implemented at the University of Michigan as changes in the learning environment that were designed to reduce the stereotype threat of African American students. Some of the changes implemented <u>included</u> optimistic teacher-student relationships, giving challenging work, stressing the "expandability of intelligence," providing role models, and building self-efficacy (Steele, 1997, p. 625). Steele (1997) <u>concluded</u> that the program was effective because these students did have higher achievement compared to similar students who <u>were</u> not in the program. This study, however, had limitations. One limitation <u>is</u> that it studied a group of African-American college students who may not accurately represent all individuals facing stereotype threats; specifically, it may be hard to <u>generalize</u> these results to all women in math and science.

3 Others have proposed guidelines and suggestions for interventions but have not empirically tested their ideas themselves. For example, in their study on predictors of high-level career choices of women, Natua et al. (1998) suggested several ideas for interventions aimed at increasing the number of women in math and science. Their ideas for interventions included increasing self-efficacy, providing role models, and reducing role conflict that the students experience, for example balancing work and family (Nauta et al.). Similarly, Gavin and Reis (2003) proposed guidelines for teachers in the classroom that are aimed at encouraging girls in math. Their guidelines <u>include</u> taking personal responsibility to encourage talented girls, creating a safe and supportive learning environment, providing single-sex learning opportunities, using language and activities that are relevant to girls, creating a challenging environment, and providing role models for girls. Both of these suggested interventions have limitations because they have not been empirically evaluated. Future studies <u>need</u> to examine the effectiveness of these intervention ideas.

[

1. Write the underlined verbs from the text in the correct column in the chart depending on what follows each verb. Note that the same verb might appear in more than one column.

Direct Object	Indirect Object (prepositional phrase)	to (infinitive) Clause	–ing Clause	that (noun) Clause

2. Write the only verb from the chart that is used in the passive voice.

_____

1.1: Clause Structure

A. A **finite clause** is at minimum a subject, a verb, and any objects or complements that the verb requires. A finite clause expresses a complete idea (*finite* means "bounded or limited") and can stand alone as a complete sentence. Table 1.1 shows the basic structure of finite clauses in English. Notice that many slots are empty but optional, whereas the shaded slots cannot be filled. This table does not show every possible combination, but it can help you analyze and control academic writing.

Table 1.1 The Slot Structure of Finite Clauses					
Adverb / Prepositional Phrase	Subject	Finite Verb	Other Verbs	Complement(s)	Adverb / Prepositional Phrase
(1)	The frequency	increased.			
(2)	Researchers	have	studied	interventions.	
(3)	The marker	gave		us additional information.	
(4) However,	the differences	can	be explained		by several factors.
(5)	Their ideas for interventions	included		increasing self-efficacy	as a first step.

B. Only the **subject** and verb slots are required in all finite clauses.[1] In affirmative statements in the present simple and past simple tenses in the active voice (Sentences 1, 3, 5), there is only one verb (that is, the **main verb** is finite), but in all other finite clauses, the verb is an **auxiliary verb**, such as *be, do, have,* or *get* and is followed by another verb (Sentence 2). Modal verbs are a type of auxiliary and can also fill the **finite verb** slot (Sentence 4) (6.1).

C. Each slot has limits on the type of word, phrase, or **clause** that can fill it. The subject slot can be a noun, pronoun, *–ing* clause, or sometimes a *to* infinitive, but not a prepositional phrase (*in the study*), an adverb (*quickly*), or a **bare infinitive** clause (*do research*).

D. Complements are the elements that come after the verb and are controlled by the verb. Different types of verbs allow or require different types of complements. For example, transitive verbs require a direct **object**, while linking verbs like *include* (Sentence 5) allow *–ing* clauses as complements, although a noun phrase would also be possible (e.g., "an increase in self-efficiency"). It is not always easy to guess which complements are possible after any particular verb; if English is not your first language, a good learner's dictionary will be very helpful.

E. **Non-finite clauses** have the same basic structure as finite clauses, but they do not have a finite verb that is bound or limited, and they do not usually have a subject. This means the verb is in the **infinitive** or *–ing* form. The complement in Sentence 5 is a non-finite clause, for example, because it has an *–ing* verb and no subject. When a non-finite clause is used as a subject or object, it is usually in the *–ing* form, although a *to* infinitive is often possible. Non-finite clauses that follow prepositions must be in the *–ing* form.

> (6a) INCORRECT: **Provide** role models was another suggestion.

> (6b) CORRECT: **Providing** role models was another suggestion.

Exercise 1: Sentence Analysis

Circle the verbs, underline the subjects, and double underline the complements in these sentences from a research report published by Johns Hopkins University about itching called "A Little to the Left" (2009) (1–5) and about microfinance, giving small loans to individuals ("Microfinance," 2010) (6–10).

1. Sensory scientists from Johns Hopkins University have discovered in mice a molecular basis for nonallergic itch.

2. Using the itch-inducing compound chloroquine, an antimalarial drug, the team identified a family of proteins called Mrgprs.

3. A report on the research appears on December 24 in *Cell*.

---

[1] The subject is required in all finite clauses *except* imperative (command) clauses. However, imperatives are unusual in academic writing, except in mathematical contexts such as *Let x denote* . . . or *Assume y is constant.*

4. There are specific nerve cells dedicated for itch, different ones for pain, and still others for pleasant touch.

5. The Mrgpr-knockout mice responded specifically to chloroquine.

6. Success or failure of microfinance depends largely on the state of a nation's economy, according to a new study.

7. Microfinance is the practice of making small loans to farmers or business owners too poor to provide collateral.

8. The microfinance movement has exploded during the past two decades.

9. Ahlin and colleagues from New York University and the University of Minnesota examined the experiences of 373 microbanks worldwide.

10. As the larger economy grew, the microbanks' profit margins grew as well.

Exercise 2: Grammatical Judgment

Which of these are correct and complete (C) finite clauses in academic writing? What is missing from or wrong in the incomplete or incorrect (I) clauses?

1.   C / I   Thirty-five seconds from start to finish.

2.   C / I   Over the centuries of development of the industrial agriculture described above.

3.   C / I   These systems damaged natural watersheds.

4.   C / I   Turning a continent of rich ecological diversity into a factory for uniform production of a few generic crops.

5.   C / I   These systems damaged.

6.   C / I   In the 1600s foreshadowed a trend in corn growing.

7.   C / I   Chicago was planned careful.

8.   C / I   The Europeans began by mapping the continent.

Exercise 3: Writing

Take a recent piece of your own writing that has not been edited or corrected. Analyze your clause and sentence structure using Table 1.1 (see page 3). Correct any errors of clause structure or word form.

1.2: Noun Phrase Structure

A. Noun phrases can be used as subjects, objects, or objects of prepositions. In academic writing, the noun phrase is often long and complex, containing the substance of the sentence. The verb may be relatively simple, but it controls the structure of the clause.

B. Like clauses, noun phrases have a structure of slots, which can be filled by different types of words. Only the main noun (called the **head noun**) is always required. Every other slot depends on the type and meaning of the head noun (see Table 1.2).

Table 1.2 The Structure of Noun Phrases						
Modifiers					*Qualifiers*	
Quantifier	Determiner	(Adverb +) Adjective(s)	Noun Modifier	Head Noun	Prepositional Phrase	(Reduced) Embedded Clause
				Florida		
			college	choice		
	a	simple dynamic		model		
	the			problem	of college choice	
a few of	the			problems		facing the panther
		initially identical		institutions		
most			Florida	panthers		

C. Notice that the noun phrases in prepositional phrases *(of college choice)* and relative clauses *(facing the panther)* follow the same sequence of slots. The noun phrase is, therefore, a very flexible element.

D. It is possible to write very long noun phrases by using all the available slots. The head nouns in Examples 7–9 are in bold.

(7) the **development** of innovative, superstrong, yet light and damage-tolerant materials

(8) the building **blocks** of larger hierarchical structures with the strength and ductility of the smaller objects

(9) the **distribution** between U.S. states of investment from countries that grant foreign tax credits

These long noun phrases are common in professional academic writing but should be used cautiously and only when the meaning is clear.

E. Identifying the head noun is especially important in the subject slot because the verb agrees with the head noun (4.8). Looking at the head noun also helps choose the correct article, *a, an, the*, if needed (articles are discussed further in Unit 5).

Exercise 4: Grammar Analysis

Circle the head noun in the underlined noun phrases from a research report by the National Institutes of Health, *How Secondhand Smoke Affects the Brain* (NIH, 2011a).

1. Tobacco is <u>the leading cause of preventable death</u> nationwide.

2. <u>Up to 90% of lung cancer deaths</u> are attributed to smoking.

3. Previous research has shown that <u>exposure to secondhand smoke</u> increases the likelihood that children will become teenage smokers.

4. <u>A team led by Dr. Arthur Brody of the University of California, Los Angeles,</u> set out to study how secondhand smoke affects the human brain.

5. The method depends on <u>a special tracer molecule</u> that binds specifically to nAChRs [nicotinic acetylcholine receptors].

6. The researchers found that <u>nAChRs in the brains of both smokers and non-smokers</u> became occupied by nicotine after 1 hour of exposure to secondhand smoke.

7. This study gives concrete evidence to support <u>policies that ban smoking in public places</u>.

Exercise 5: Sentence Completion

Underline the head noun and draw an arrow to its verb. Then circle the correct form of the verb in parentheses to complete each sentence.

1. Considering the relative youth of the environmental justice movement in the United States, as well as the ingrained racial tensions and discrimination practices that (exists / exist) in the U.S. as opposed to many other countries, it may come as a surprise to some that the environmental justice movement (is / are) not a social movement unique to the United States.

2. Environmental problems that citizens in the United States (faces / face) (shares / share) one major similarity with those in Southeast Asia: both movements (is / are) almost always addressing a negative change to the status quo.

3. One problem that (tends / tend) to be very different between the cases in Southeast Asia as ompared to cases in the United States (is / are) this idea of land use vs. land preservation.

4. The second way that U.S. environmental justice problems often (differs / differ) from those in Southeast Asia (has / have) to do with the nature of the problems themselves.

5. Many of the victims of environmental injustices in Southeast Asia (loses / lose) their land, their homes, or their occupation when they give way to government or industry.

6. The all-important link between the causes of environmental justice issues both domestically and in developing countries (is / are) that industry and government often have shared interest in pursuing the path of least resistance.

1.3: Word Form

A. Many words exist in families of nouns, verbs, adjective, and adverbs. Many words do not have all four family members, while others have one form for two family members or two or more different words for one family member (Table 1.3).

Table 1.3 Word Families			
Noun	**Verb**	**Adjective**	**Adverb**
experience	experience	experiential experienced	experientially
consideration	consider	considerate	considerately
research researcher	research		

B. Related words can be quite different in meaning; for example, *considerate* means "kind or compassionate" and is only loosely related to the verb *consider*, meaning "to think about."

C. Other parts of speech include prepositions (*at, to, on, above, against*), **pronouns** (*I, me, my, mine*), and conjunctions (*because, when, if*). Even these words can have multiple functions: *since* can be a preposition (*since 2005*) or a conjunction (*since records began*).

D. It is important to choose the right word form because some slots in the clause or noun phrase are limited to certain parts of speech.

1. The subject of a clause cannot be a prepositional phrase, adverb, or adjective.[2]

    (10a) INCORRECT: **In the United States** are approximately 1,300 cases of malaria annually.

    (10b) CORRECT: In the United States, **there** are approximately 1,300 cases of malaria annually.

2. Adverbs can modify adjectives but not nouns.

    (11a) INCORRECT: The university is subject to **quickly** changes in the environment.

    (11b) CORRECT: The university is subject to **quick** changes in the environment.

---

[2] There is a possible and rare exception. With certain linking verbs (such as *be,*) the complement can be moved to the subject position for special effect; for example, *Typical is the following description,* meaning "the following description is typical."

3. Adverbs can modify most verbs, adjectives, and clauses, but not usually linking verbs such as *be* (1.7).

   (12a) INCORRECT: It is **clearly** that bioethanol is not a final solution.

   (12b) CORRECT: It is **clear** that bioethanol is not a final solution.

   (12c) CORRECT: Bioethanol is **clearly** not a final solution.

4. Non-finite verbs (i.e., in the *–ing* or *to* infinitive forms) can be used as subjects, but not finite or base forms (the base form is the infinitive without *to*).

   (13a) INCORRECT: **Understand** this phenomenon is important for many reasons.

   (13b) CORRECT: **Understanding** this phenomenon is important for many reasons.

5. A noun phrase cannot consist of an article plus an adjective.

   (14a) INCORRECT: The experiment was **a successful**.

   (14b) CORRECT: The experiment was **a success**.

   (14c) CORRECT: The experiment was **successful**.

Exercise 6: Grammatical Judgment

Choose the best form of the word in parentheses to complete the sentences.

1. Many factors need to be in place, including (adequate / adequately) resources.

2. The authors of this study (analysis / analyze / analytic) a (national / nationally) representative sample of undergraduate students.

3. Two kinds of (guarantee / guaranteed) are possible. One is (guarantee / guaranteed) employment for everyone who is willing to work (conscientious / conscientiously).

4. There was a slight (decrease / decreased / decreasing) trend.

5. The phenomenon is a (widespread / challenge / perceive).

Exercise 7: Sentence Writing

Write sentences using these words that are often confused. Do not change the form.

1. against _____

2. interested _____

3. lack _____

4. including _____

5. aware _____

6. access _____

7. priority _____

8. concern _____

1.4 Verbs and Complements

A. Verbs can be categorized by their meaning. Different types of verbs describe different kinds of experiences: **Action verbs** describe events, **reporting verbs** report speech and ideas, and **linking verbs** show how things are related. Each type of verb allows or requires different types of subjects and complements.[3] Therefore, the choice of verb controls the structure of the clause. Table 1.4 on page 11 summarizes common clause patterns in both active and passive voice. The patterns are described in 1.5–1.7.

---

[3] This classification is adapted and much simplified from Halliday (1994, Ch. 5). Specifically, material and behavioral processes have been conflated into action verbs and verbal and mental processes into reporting verbs. For a detailed description of functional grammar's "processes" (verb types), see Eggins, 2004, or Lock, 1995.

Table 1.4 Common Clause Patterns		
	Active Voice Patterns	**Passive Voice Patterns (4.6)**
Action Verbs		
• *Intransitive* (1.5)	S + V (+ adverb/prepositional phrase) *An unusual reaction occurred (in the glass).* agent	
• *Transitive* (1.5)	S + V + DO *His team designed the system.* agent　　　　　goal	S + V (+ *by* phrase) *The system was designed (by his team).* goal　　　　　　　agent
• *Ditransitive (double object)* (1.5)	S + V + DO + IO *The government sold land to settlers.* agent　　　　　　goal　recipient S + V + IO + DO *The government sold　them　land.* agent　　　　　　　recipient　goal	S + V + DO (+ *by* phrase) *Settlers　were sold land (by the government).* recipient　　　goal　　　agent S + V + IO (+ *by* phrase) *Land was sold to settlers (by the government).* goal　　　　recipient　　　agent
Reporting Verbs (1.6, 3.3, 3.5)	S + V + DO *Table 1 shows the results.* S + V + noun clause *Table 1 shows that the results are significant.* S + V + -*ing* non-finite clause *The picture shows the researcher conducting the test.* S + V + *to* non-finite clause *Table 1 shows the results to be significant.*	S + V + *to* non-finite clause *The product is known to be dangerous.* It + V + noun clause *It is known that the product is dangerous*
Linking Verbs (1.7, 2.4, 3.5)	S + V + subject complement *The operation lasted two hours.* S + V + noun clause *It appears that the test was successful.* It + V + *to* non-finite clause *The experiment appears to be finished.* It is + adjective (+ for s/o) + *to* clause *It is important for scientists to behave ethically.* It is + adjective + noun clause *It is clear that further research is needed.*	S + V + subject complement *The process is called fossilization.*

Notes: S = subject; V = verb; DO = direct object (an object without a preposition); IO = indirect object (an object that usually requires a preposition); s/o = *someone*.

1.5 Action Verbs

A. When an action verb is used, something (the **agent**) acts upon something (the **goal**), sometimes for something else (the **recipient**). The terms *agent, goal,* and *recipient* describe the function of a word in the clause.

B. Most action verbs are **transitive** and have both an agent and a goal, although the agent is often omitted in the passive voice (see 4.6). Very few verbs are truly **intransitive**, meaning they have no goal and cannot be followed by a **direct object**. Many intransitive verbs also have a transitive form or are used with a prepositional phrase or adverb that could be considered an **indirect object**.

> (15) The experiment **started**.   *(intransitive)*
>
> (16) We **started** the experiment. *(transitive)*
>
> (17) We **listened** to the interviews. *(required prepositional phrase)*

There is a difference in meaning between Sentences 15 and 16. When the verb *start* is transitive (Sentence 16), there is a human agent that causes the experiment (the goal) to start. The experiment appears to start by itself when the verb is intransitive (Sentence 15). Using a non-human agent can be very useful if you write in a discipline that discourages the use of personal pronouns (*I* and *we*).

C. A small number of verbs are **ditransitive**, or double-object verbs (Table 1.4). This means they allow an indirect object that identifies the recipient of the action. These verbs have the basic meaning of *give*, such as *leave, bring, show, tell, lend,* or *sell*.

Exercise 8: Sentence Completion

Complete each sentence with an object, a prepositional phrase, or an adverb. More than one answer is possible. Compare your sentences with a partner. Discuss your decisions.

Example: The number of voters increased _from 2000-2008_.
                  The number of voters increased _the cost of holding elections_.

1. The company grew _____.

2. The change created _____.

3. The book was published _____.

4. The city recycles _____.

5. We collected _____.

Exercise 9: Sentence Writing

Write sentences using these verbs. Use passive or active voice, and change the verb tense as needed.

1. send _____

2. apply _____

3. change _____

4. understand _____

5. reduce _____

6. contribute _____

7. provide _____

8. end _____

9. create _____

10. describe _____

Exercise 10: Writing

Think of someone who has the job you want to have eventually (a professor, a manager, a professional, or a researcher). Describe what that person does in that position. Use a variety of intransitive, transitive, and ditransitive verbs with appropriate voice, objects, and complements. Then exchange your paragraph with a partner who is not familiar with the job you chose. Read your partner's paper and ask questions about any content you do not understand. Look at all the verbs and check the clause structure together.

1.6 Reporting Verbs

A. Reporting verbs describe what people say, think, feel, or want. Although they are commonly followed by noun clauses (3.3), other complements are possible with certain verbs. It can be difficult to predict which of the patterns in Table 1.4 are possible for individual verbs. The patterns for some common verbs are provided in Table 1.5.

Table 1.5 Complements of Common Saying/Thinking Verbs in the Active Voice				
	Noun Phrase	**Finite Noun Clause**	***-ing* Clause**	***to* Infinitive Clause**
suggest	He suggested a solution.	He suggested that we do it.	He suggested doing something.	
recommend	I recommend the book.	I recommend that you buy the book.	I recommend buying the book.	I recommend you to buy the book.[4]
claim	We claim victory.	We claim that we have succeeded.		We claim to have succeeded.
show	Table 1 shows the results.	Table 1 shows that the results are significant.	The illustration shows the researcher conducting the test.	Table 1 shows the results to be significant.

B. When you have a choice between clause structures, consider these principles:

1. Using a finite clause often produces a longer sentence than using a non-finite clause and is grammatically more complex. Non-finite clauses are often preferred in academic writing (Biber et al., 1999, p. 755).

2. Some choices permit or require the introduction of an indirect object (*I recommend **you** to buy the book*). This can improve clarity but may be inappropriate in some academic fields.

3. Some choices can reduce redundancy by omitting unnecessary participants (*We claim to have succeeded* is more concise but expresses the same idea as *We claim that we have succeeded*).

---

[4] This sentence pattern appears to be rare.

C. Some saying/thinking verbs allow or require an indirect object. Thus, the choice of verb also affects the amount and type of information that can be included in the clause. Some of the most common reporting verbs in academic writing are summarized in Table 1.6.

Table 1.6 Indirect Objects with Saying/Thinking Verbs			
No Indirect Object	**Required Indirect Object (no preposition)**	**Optional Indirect Object (without preposition)**	**Optional Indirect Object (with preposition)**
believe, think, wonder, realize, notice, discover, find, assume, suspect, doubt, recommend, note, answer, add	*tell, convince, inform, persuade, remind*	*show, teach, warn, promise, caution, ask, write* [5]	*agree (with), say (to), prove (to), admit (to), argue (with), explain (to), claim (to), suggest (to), comment (to), maintain (to), observe (to), point out (to), report (to), respond (to)*
(18) The social worker **realized** that the mother was extremely skeptical.	(19) One other [grant] tries to **persuade** students that cheating is wrong.	(20) The results **show** **that** this option is not a realistic alternative. (21) We need to **show** children that there can be mixed emotions.	(22) Most models **agree** that elevated temperatures will decrease soil moisture. (23) We must also **agree** with him that it is confusing and misleading.

Exercise 11: Error Correction

Correct the error in each sentence.

1. The report implied us that changes were needed.

2. We convinced to try the new restaurant.

3. The CEO denied to lie about the company's finances.

4. The authors suggested to reform the tax code.

5. The effect was estimated large.

---

[5] *Write* can take an indirect object without a preposition in American English, but not in some other varieties, including British English (e.g., *I wrote [British: to] him that I was coming*).

Exercise 12: Sentence Rewriting

Rewrite these sentences in the passive voice.

1. We believe that international students bring a lot of money to the state.

   It _____.

2. Some people say that consumers are more cost-conscious these days.

   Consumers _____.

3. Many people claim that illegal immigrants take jobs from citizens.

   It _____.

4. We know that fast food is one cause of obesity in young people.

   Fast food _____.

5. Experts suspect that some pesticides cause diseases in humans.

   It _____.

1.7 Linking Verbs

A. Linking verbs do not describe any action or event. Instead, they express what something *is* or *is related to*. They are frequently used in academic and scientific writing because they allow writers to link one concept (usually a noun phrase) to a value, fact, or idea.

> (24) The operation **lasted** two hours.

> (25) The rate **remained** stable.

> (26) The proportion of the Chinese population with tertiary education **has always been** small relative to the entire population.

B. The complement of a linking verb is called a subject complement because it complements—or adds to the meaning of—the subject. The **complement** may take many forms, depending on the meaning of the clause, but it must always be equivalent to the subject in some sense.

> (27a) INCORRECT: Reactions to the new policy were variety.

> (27b) CORRECT: Reactions to the new policy were varied.

It is correct to describe reactions as varied (Sentence 27b), but the reactions are not a variety of anything (Sentence 27a).

C. Some linking verbs describe a characteristic of the subject (Eggins, 2004, p. 240), such as *be, have, become, turn (into / out), keep, stay, remain, seem, grow, appear, look, sound, feel, measure, weigh, cost, ensure, vary (in),* and *differ (in).* These verbs are not usually written in the passive voice.

(28) The results seem **clear**.

(29) The size of the sample became **an important consideration**.

D. Another function of linking verbs is to link a word to its definition or to a statement about its identity (Eggins, 2004, p. 241). Some common verbs are: *be, have, mean, suggest, show, represent, define, indicate, correspond to, constitute, resemble, refer to, reflect, comprise, feature, make, illustrate, express, stand for, name, call, prove, consider, signify,* and *act as.* When functioning in this way, linking verbs may be used in the passive voice.

(30) *C* **refers to** the cost of the product.

(31) The reasons **include** the increase in demographic diversity.

(32) The process **is called** fossilization.

(33) The demand for gas **is represented by** the symbol *d*.

E. Linking verbs sometimes take noun clauses as complements. However, the common verbs *appear* and *seem* can also use *it* as an **empty subject** (Sentence 36).

(34) The data **indicate** that the condition is genetic.

(35) One explanation **is** that higher drug use prompts more frequent testing.

(36) It **appears/seems** that the new policy is effective. *[The new policy appears/seems effective.]*

Exercise 13: Sentence Completion

Replace the verb *be* or complete each sentence with an appropriate verb from the box. Change the form of the verb if necessary. More than one answer is possible.

appear	include	mean	stand for
define	last	remain	vary

1. A recession can <u>be</u> many years.

2. Unemployment can <u>be</u> high for months after a recession.

3. According to economists, a recession <u>is</u> two consecutive quarters of negative growth.

4. It <u>is not</u> that everyone suffers during a recession.

5. GDP <u>is</u> gross domestic product.

6. An increase in the exchange rate _____ that the price of domestic goods will be more expensive relative to foreign goods.

7. The economic problems facing the country <u>are</u> the high level of debt and the fall in manufacturing.

8. Experts _____ in their solutions to these problems.

Exercise 14: Writing

Choose a technical term, theory, or piece of equipment from your field of study. Write several sentences to define and describe it using different linking verbs in each sentence. Remember to avoid repeating the verb *be* too often. Then exchange sentences with a partner and check that the meaning and grammar are clear.

1.8 Three Levels of Meaning

A. Writers can often choose between different clause structures and word forms.

> (37a) Some people say that consumers are spending less money.

> (37b) Consumers are said to be spending less money.

> (37c) Consumers appear to be spending less money.

In one way, these three sentences have the same meaning because they describe the same phenomenon. However, the sentences also have different meanings: Sentence 37a focuses on *some people*, while the other two are exclusively about consumers. Sentences 37a and 37b put responsibility for the claim on someone else, whereas the writer takes more responsibility for the claim in Sentence 37c.

B. Linguists who follow Halliday's "**functional grammar**" (Halliday, 1994) explain this phenomenon by arguing that grammar creates three layers of meaning simultaneously:

1. facts, things, and experiences (**experiential** meaning—what happened?)
2. your attitudes and evaluations (**interpersonal** meaning—what do you think about it?)
3. the organization of the text (**textual meaning**—how will you present it?)

Therefore, Sentences 37a–c all had similar experiential meaning but different interpersonal and textual meanings because the message was organized differently and the sentences showed different levels of confidence in the claim about consumers.

C. Functional grammar, which underlies the approach to grammar taken in this textbook, is interested in what grammar *does* in your writing (its functions), rather than what it *is* (the "rules" of grammar). As you write, you are making choices at all three levels of meaning all the time. For example, consider these sentences.

> (38a) This study gives concrete evidence to support policies that ban smoking in public places.
>
> (38b) Concrete evidence supports policies that ban smoking in public places.
>
> (38c) A ban on smoking in public places is supported by evidence from this study.
>
> (38d) This study tells us that smoking should be banned in public places.

Again, the experiential meaning is similar in all four sentences, but a writer might choose each sentence for different reasons. Looking at organization first (the textual meaning), Sentences 38a and 38d are about the study, Sentence 38b focuses on the evidence, and Sentence 38c talks directly about the ban on smoking. Notice the choice of the passive voice in Sentence 38c, which allows the writer to move the evidence to the end of the sentence, where it might be developed in further sentences (8.1). In terms of interpersonal meaning, the choice of *tells* in Sentence 38d introduces an indirect object (*us*), making the sentence more conversational and less appropriate for most academic contexts. Sentence 38b seems most direct, using *supports* as an action verb without mentioning the source of the evidence.

Exercise 15: Sentence Rewriting

Experiment with the three layers of meaning by rewriting the sentences as suggested. Discuss your choices.

1. Increased natural resource use has negatively impacted the environment.

    a. (change the textual meaning)

        The environment has been negatively impacted by natural resource use.

    b. (change the interpersonal meaning by adding a modal verb)

        _____.

2. The United States holds a very small fraction of total world resource reserves, but we account for a disproportionately large fraction of total resource consumption.

    a. (change the interpersonal meaning by rewriting without *we*)

        _____.

    b. (change the experiential meaning by rewriting about another country)

        _____.

    c. (change the textual meaning by changing the order of the two clauses)

        _____.

3. Reserves of oil are expected to last 36 years.

    a. (change the interpersonal meaning by rewriting without the reporting verb *expect*)

        _____.

    b. (change the interpersonal and textual meaning by starting *Scientists expect*)

        _____.

    c. (change the interpersonal and experiential meaning by rewriting with an action verb such as *exhaust* or *run out*)

        _____.

Grammar in Your Discipline

A. Look through an article or book in your discipline and find examples of:

1. an action verb with one participant (an intransitive verb)

2. an action verb with three participants (a ditransitive verb)

3. an action verb in the passive voice

4. a passive verb with the agent in the *by* phrase (this might be hard to find)

B. Look again at your texts and answer these questions.

1. What are some frequently used *reporting* verbs? _____

   _____

2. Examine the indirect objects (if relevant) and types of complements (noun phrase, finite clause, *to / –ing* clause of the reporting verbs). Do you notice any patterns or surprises? _____

   _____

3. Which types of verbs appear to be most common: action, reporting, or linking? Can you explain why? _____

   _____

C. Share your findings with a small group of writers from other disciplines. Do you notice any similarities or differences? If you are using *Academic Writing for Graduate Students*, compare your findings for B1 to Table 15 on page 213.

D. Write a summary of a journal or magazine article you have read recently. Edit your summary carefully for clause structure.

For more information about summary writing, see Unit 5 of *Academic Writing for Graduate Students*, 3rd edition.

Clause Combination

Although a sentence can be written with just one finite clause, writers often combine clauses to form compound and complex sentences. The types of clause and combining forms that are chosen affect the way the message is controlled. Unit 2 introduces two types of clause combinations, which will be called **equal** clauses (coordination) and **unequal** clauses (some types of subordination).

UNIT 2 Preview Test

Determine whether each sentence is acceptable in formal, academic written English. Write Y for yes or N for no. Discuss your choices.

_____ 1. The variation of language in society.

_____ 2. To explain the difference between British and American English.

_____ 3. Sociolinguistics, it is the study of language variation in society.

_____ 4. There are two main types of linguistic variation, the first identifies people within certain groups.

_____ 5. For example, American English, British English, or Australian English.

_____ 6. There are many varieties of English, however most English speakers can understand each other.

_____ 7. Although, there can be misunderstandings.

_____ 8. Grammar, however, is always more difficult.

Grammar Awareness: Definition

Read this definition of folk tales from a paper written for an English literature class (included in MICUSP) and complete the tasks.

For Zipes, fairy tales and folk tales reflect the values of a society, // (and) his essay clearly demonstrates an attempt to locate fairy tales within their social and historical context // while specifically highlighting the effects of fairy tales // as designed by Walt Disney. Zipes places the folk tale securely in the realm of the community, as stories are passed down from generation to generation without written record. In this way, storytelling was the product of communal efforts, and folk tales thus reflected the values of an entire society and provided a means to teach those values to children. The invention of the printing press and the rise of literary folk tales resulted in sanitized versions of traditional tales for children, although fairy tales were not deemed entirely appropriate for children until the late eighteenth and early nineteenth centuries. For a time, then, the printing press actually decreased the accessibility of fairy tales to children. Furthermore, these printed texts were generally accessible only to the wealthy. This resulted in an overall shift in the reception of fairy tales; an oral, communal activity became more heavily focused upon the private realm, although oral traditions did continue to an extent. These two divergent traditions resulted in a greater social schism, as the literary fairy tale was reserved for the elite and the oral folk tale largely became a tradition of the lower classes. As Zipes argues, however, industrialization itself was not completely negative since literary rates spread and the standard of living generally improved.

1. Divide the sentences into clauses by inserting slash marks (//). The first one has been done as an example. Explain to a partner how you chose to divide the text.

2. Circle the words used to connect clauses. Look for coordinating conjunctions, subordinating conjunctions, and sentence connectors.

2.1 Types of Clauses

A. A clause is an idea that is organized around a verb. Recall from Unit 1 that a finite clause has a subject that agrees with the verb. A finite clause can be a complete sentence in written English; for this reason it is called an **independent** or **main clause**.

> (1) Tuition is expensive.

B. A clause that cannot stand alone as a complete sentence is called a **dependent clause** because it depends on an independent clause to form a grammatical sentence. Dependent clauses may be finite or non-finite. A finite clause has a subject and finite verb, whereas a non-finite clause is built around a *to* infinitive or *–ing* verb. A summary of English clauses is shown in Figure 2.1.

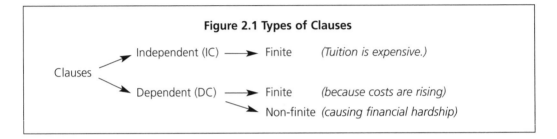

Figure 2.1 Types of Clauses

Clauses
- Independent (IC) → Finite *(Tuition is expensive.)*
- Dependent (DC) → Finite *(because costs are rising)*
- → Non-finite *(causing financial hardship)*

C. A single independent clause can form a sentence, called a **simple sentence**. Since it typically has one main verb, the simple sentence essentially expresses one idea—for example, an action, event, state, or link between two things. Simple sentences are not always short and can contain a lot of information.

> (2) Social network sites **arose** in the late 1990s.
>
> (3) According to a Nielsen Online report, by the end of 2008, some 66.8 percent of Internet users around the world **had visited** social network sites that year.

D. When it is necessary to develop ideas, show logical relationships, add conditions or concessions, or refer to a source, combinations of clauses are often used. One option is to start a new sentence with a sentence connector such as *however* or *therefore* (see Table 2.1 on page 26).

> (4) Online social networks generate revenues through advertising. **Indeed**, advertisers use these sites to create targeted ads to reach particular customers.

E. Multiple clauses can be combined into one sentence. The patterns in which clauses can combine are fairly flexible, which allows writers a great deal of choice and control over the organization of meaning. These patterns are not just different in grammar and punctuation; they also express different logical relationships between the clauses.

Exercise 1: Grammar Awareness

This paragraph is an excerpt from a student's definition of malaria. Indicate whether each numbered clause is independent (IC) or dependent (DC).

❶ Malaria is caused by a parasite with the genus *Plasmodium*. ❷ There are only four known species of *Plasmodium* ❸ that cause malaria. ❹ Malaria is transmitted by female mosquitoes of the genus *Anopheles*. ❺ There are over 430 known genus species of *Anopheles*, ❻ but only about 30–50 of them can actually transmit the parasite. ❼ Normally malaria is a curable disease, ❽ if treated properly. ❾ After an infectious bite, ❿ there is an incubation period in the host ⓫ that varies ⓬ depending on the species of *Plasmodium*.

1. _____   7. _____

2. _____   8. _____

3. _____   9. _____

4. _____   10. _____

5. _____   11. _____

6. _____   12. _____

2.2 Equal and Unequal Clauses

A. When two independent clauses of equal status are combined, they are both equally important to the message. The first clause starts the message, and the other continues it. A sentence with two independent clauses is called a **compound sentence**.

(5) Network members can post news, photographs, videos, and other content, **and** they can share this material with designated recipients.

(6) Analysts emphasize that network members should be extremely careful in communicating with strangers online; people can lie about who they really are.

B. Compound sentences can be created in two ways.

1. Join two independent clauses with a **coordinating conjunction** (see Table 2.1). Insert a comma before the **conjunction**.

2. Join two independent clauses with a semi-colon. A sentence connector may be used in the second clause.

C. In other types of sentences, the clauses are unequal. These are formed by using a combination of independent and dependent clauses. The independent clause contains the main idea of the sentence, and the dependent clause, finite or non-finite, modifies the main clause by expanding its meaning. This does not mean it is less important than the main clause; the dependent clause adds meaning to the main clause and may contain essential new information (8.1). A sentence with an independent and a dependent clause is one type of **complex sentence**.

(7) Potential employers have been known to check a person's MySpace or Facebook profile **before** they decide to make a hire.

(8) Cybercriminals can gain access to sensitive information from online social networks, **making** users vulnerable to identity theft and other crimes.

(9) Other kinds of malicious behavior include bullying, **which** can take many forms.

The placement of dependent clauses is flexible. Most dependent clauses can also precede the main clause.

(10) **Though particular details differ**, these networks generally offer members the opportunity to share personal information with a selected group of "friends."

(11) **Posing as legitimate users,** criminals can use online networks to gain access to potential victims.

D. Complex sentences can be created four ways.

1. Combine an independent clause and a dependent clause with a **subordinating conjunction** (see Table 2.1).

2. Combine an independent clause with a non-restrictive relative clause (2.3).

3. Combine an independent clause with an *–ing* clause (a reduced non-restrictive relative clause) (2.4).

4. Embed a relative or noun clause in an independent clause (Unit 3).

Table 2.1 Conjunctions and Sentence Connectors		
Coordinating conjunctions *form equal clauses.*	**Subordinating conjunctions** *form unequal clauses.*	**Sentence connectors** *start new independent clauses or sentences.*
for and nor but } = FANBOYS or yet so	as because although (even) though if when while unless even if before after etc.	as a result therefore however nevertheless instead also too then for example / for instance on the other hand thus etc.

Exercise 2: Paragraph Completion

Complete the passage from the National Institutes of Health (2011b) with conjunctions and sentence connectors from Table 2.1.

Weighing In on Dietary Fats:
Some Fats Are Healthier Than Others

❶ _____ the winter holidays arrive, you'll likely be surrounded by family, friends, and plenty of good food. Many of these foods,

❷ _____, can be high in fat. ❸ _____ you learn which fats are naughty and which are nice to your health, ❹ _____ you can make smarter food choices.

We need a certain amount of fat in our diets to stay healthy. Fats provide needed energy in the form of calories, ❺ _____ they help our bodies absorb important vitamins, ❻ _____ Vitamins A, D, and E. Fats ❼ _____ make foods more flavorful and help us feel full. Fats are especially important for infants and toddlers ❽ _____ dietary fat contributes to proper growth and development.

Problems arise, ❾ _____, from eating too much fat ❿ _____ eating the wrong kinds of fats. Unsaturated fats are considered "good" fats. These can promote health ⓫ _____ eaten in the right amounts. They are generally liquid at room temperature ⓬ _____ are known as oils. ⓭ _____, "bad" saturated fats and trans fats tend to be solid at room temperature.

Exercise 3: Sentence Writing

Continue each sentence using a different conjunction or connector from Table 2.1. Punctuate your writing carefully.

1. Driving can be dangerous _____.

2. Air travel has become less convenient _____.

3. High-speed trains have been highly successful in some countries _____.

4. Electric vehicles may be the future of personal travel _____.

5. The price of oil is expected to increase _____.

2.3 Non-Restrictive Relative Clauses

A. There are two types of relative clauses, but they function very differently. **Restrictive relative clauses** are part of the noun phrase and are discussed further in Unit 3. On the other hand, a **non-restrictive relative clause** is an important type of unequal clause.

B. Non-restrictive relative clauses elaborate on the meaning of something in the main clause with additional information, clarifications, descriptions, explanations, or comments. The "something" is known as the **referent** and can be a single noun, an idea, or the entire clause (Sentence 13).

> (12) Children's transition to formal schooling generally occurs at age 5 in the United States when children move from preschool to kindergarten**, which is the start of elementary school**. [*which = kindergarten;* the relative clause defines kindergarten in terms of the school system]
>
> (13) It is axiomatic that America wants to be loved**, which suggests that we are not loved as much as we would like.**

C. Non-restrictive clauses are always separated from the main clause with commas to show that they are connected logically and not embedded (3.1).

D. In some cases, the non-restrictive clause contains new information (8.1), especially when it appears at the end of the sentence, the typical position for new information. These clauses extend the main clause with a result, suggestion, or implication. Very often, such clauses are reduced (2.4).

E. A relative clause introduced by a quantifier such as *most of, some of,* or *two of* is always non-restrictive and requires at least one comma depending on its location. In addition, only the pronouns *which* (for non-human referents) and *whom* (for human referents) are used (not *that* or *who*) after quantifiers.

>   (14) The college has three campuses**, two of which were represented in this study.**
>
>   (15) The change in these students**, some of whom never spent an overnight outside before,** is remarkable.

These clauses are non-restrictive because they add clarification about the referent noun; they do not define or qualify it. For example, in Sentence 14, the study looked at two campuses, which does not change the fact that the college has three campuses.

Exercise 4: Sentence Completion

Complete these sentences with non-restrictive relative clauses.

1. The Internet, which _____

   _____.

2. Many regional newspapers have gone bankrupt, which _____

   _____.

3. International students, who _____

   _____.

4. International students, some of _____

   _____.

5. There are many ways to solve the problem of _____, one of _____

   _____.

6. Most doctoral students have to write a dissertation, which _____

   _____.

7. Albert Einstein, who _____

   _____.

8. Many people were affected by the 2008 economic downturn, which _____

   _____.

2.4 *–ing* Clauses

A. When a non-restrictive relative clause is at the end of a sentence, it can often be reduced to an *–ing* clause. The relative pronoun (*which* or *who*) is omitted, and the verb is changed from a finite form to the *–ing* **non-finite verb** form. This structure is especially useful for clauses of result, such as *resulting in, leading to,* and *causing,* or for explanations using verbs such as *suggesting, meaning,* and *implying.*

> (16) MRSA[1] infections total approximately two million annually, **resulting in** approximately 90,000 deaths and $4.5 billion in health care costs.

B. The adverbs *thus, therefore,* and (less commonly) *thereby* may be added before the *–ing* verb. Since the dependent clause is non-finite, this does not create a run-on (2.7).

> (17) Economies of scale can be achieved, **thus reducing** the cost to the consumer.

Unit 3 of *Academic Writing for Graduate Students,* 3rd edition, discusses the use of *–ing* clauses in problem-solution texts.

C. An *-ing* clause can also function as the subject of a finite clause and the object of a preposition.

> (18) **Restoring** devastated mangrove forests has proven difficult.

> (19) The aim of this project is to evaluate the feasibility **of providing** the university with renewable energy.

---

[1] MRSA (methicillin-resistant *Staphylococcus aureus*)—a bacterium that is resistant to antibiotics, causing a life-threatening disease.

Exercise 5: Sentence Combination

Make changes to combine each pair of sentences by using an –*ing* clause.

1. MRSA has recently been found to be capable of penetrating intact skin.

   This allows the bacteria to infect deeper layers of tissue.

2. Thirty-four pairs of students participated in this condition.

   This resulted in 17 tests for scoring and analysis.

3. Clean air standards were tightened.

   Thus the advantage of gas as a fuel was increased.

4. Teacher-librarians want to provide excellent quality resources.

   This has always been a goal of teacher-librarians.

5. Consumers may be reluctant to look to smaller or lesser-known suppliers.

   In this way, they create a smaller market.

6. Much less political attention has focused on the more controversial idea.

   This idea promotes policies that increase efficiency within the fishing sector.

Exercise 6: Sentence Completion

Complete each sentence with an –*ing* clause and your own ideas.

1. The _____ is falling, meaning _____

   _____.

2. There are many problems with _____, including

   _____.

3. _____

   is a new challenge for _____.

4. Many students have difficulty with _____.

5. _____ has become an important part of

   _____.

2.5 Logic and Clause Combination

A. Using both equal and unequal clauses **expands** a sentence, but it is important to choose carefully between them. For example, sentences with subordinators are sometimes clearer than sentences joined with coordinating conjunctions because they distinguish between the main idea and the modifying idea. If both clauses are equal in importance, it is not always easy to follow the development of the ideas. Coordinating conjunctions should not, therefore, be overused. Research has also shown that proficient writers do not use sentence connectors very frequently (Hinkel, 2004) but prefer other forms of cohesion and paragraph development (8.4).

B. There are three basic categories of meaning created by these clauses: elaborating, extending, and enhancing (Halliday, 1994, p. 225). Halliday gives the useful metaphor of a house. If you want to improve your house, you can add to the existing structure (**elaborating**), make it bigger by building more rooms (**extending**), or improve its appearance (**enhancing**).

C. **Elaborating** clauses do not add new information, but rather describe or comment on the main clause. The sentence connectors and linking phrases *for example, in particular, in other words, in fact, actually, indeed,* and *that is (i.e.)* allow writers to elaborate, as do non-restrictive relative clauses, which can describe or "gloss" (define) a word or clause.

> (20) Today, students are no longer flocking to universities; **in fact,** the United States struggles to produce enough scientists, technologists, engineers, and mathematicians.

> (21) Their populations are continuing to grow **and indeed** are expected to increase by 475 million between now and 2050.

> (22) Most public library cards enable you to access high-end, online subscription databases**, which are** immensely richer than typical Web freebies.

D. **Extension** means the writer is adding new information. This could be achieved with the coordinating conjunctions *and, but, yet, or,* and *nor,* or the sentence connectors *in addition, also, moreover* (for addition), and *conversely, alternatively, on the other hand* (for alternatives). Certain subordinating conjunctions can introduce an alternative to the main clause, for example, *while* or *whereas.* The prepositions *besides, apart from, instead of, rather than, except for,* and *as well as* can also be used as phrase linkers.

> (23) Studies are needed in which surveys are counterbalanced for question order and administered in multiple contexts. **Moreover,** it is necessary for researchers to report question order and survey context in their methods sections.

> (24) The traditional method of schooling was centered on the teacher and the textbook, **whereas** Dewey's method focused on the individual student.

E. Enhancing a clause means expanding the meaning of the main clause with time, place, manner, cause/effect, concessions, or conditions (Halliday, 1994, p. 232). Most coordinating conjunctions can express enhancement: *and* (the next event), *for* (the reason), *yet* (a concession), and *so* (a result). Many sentence connectors can also be used for enhancement: *meanwhile* (at the same time), *therefore* (result), and *otherwise* (negative consequence). Subordinating conjunctions express conditions (*if, unless*), concessions (*even though, although*), reasons (*because*), time (*before, after, when, while, since*), or manner (*as if, like*).

(25) Risk taking is not a safe option, **so** taking the sure and easy path is the only choice.

(26) **Unless** they make greater efforts, the legacy built by the baby boomers is in danger.

F. Some writers confuse *even though* and *even if. Even though* and *although* express a relationship of concession and are often accompanied by the adverb *still. Even though* means the writer accepts the idea in the dependent clause, but still believes the main clause is true. *Even if* introduces a conditional clause (6.4), which may or may not be true, but the main clause remains true.

(27) The processes are similar in both situations **even though** the products achieve different goals.

(28) Large effects could be seen **even if** the temperature increases are relatively small.

G. The sentence connector *on the other hand* is not identical in meaning to *however*. It is only used to indicate a direct contrast, such as an opposing viewpoint or alternate possibility. *However* is used for a concession, problem, or disagreement or sometimes to indicate an unexpected result or consequence.

(29) One could argue that reproduction is a non-essential life function and thus would be turned off when resources are in low supply. **On the other hand**, in terms of evolution the success of an organism is measured by its genetic contribution to the future.

(30) These areas then become prone to fire. **However,** there have also been short-term successes.

(31) Almost all studies have found positive earnings gains from an associate's degree, with an average estimate across the studies of 13 percent for males and 22 percent for females. **However**, these estimates rely on data from only five surveys.

Exercise 7: Clause Combination

Read these sentences adapted from a definition and explanation of Internet plagiarism (Hricko, 1998). Combine each set of clauses and sentences using a logical connector. Punctuate correctly.

1. Internet plagiarism has become an increasing concern for educators. Strategies to deter this latest form of academic misconduct must be developed.

   _____

   _____

2. Educators must implement proactive approaches in the teaching and prevention of such behavior. They must first re-examine the university's existing policy on plagiarism.

   _____

   _____

3. More students use the Internet for research. The temptation to plagiarize has greatly increased.

   _____

   _____

4. Students can refer to any search engine. They can quickly retrieve a number of websites that offer full text information ready to be copied.

   _____

   _____

   _____

5. Most universities have established policies to respond to plagiarism. Some instructors do not take time to review this material with their students.

   _____

   _____

   _____

6. Plagiarism can occur in any classroom. It is pertinent that *all* instructors review the existing policy on plagiarism at the beginning of each new term. The course they teach is not writing intensive.

   _____

   _____

   _____

7. University policy should first define plagiarism. The university should offer an explanation on the types of offenses that can be considered forms of academic misconduct.

_____

_____

_____

8. Most university webpages include sections that outline the school's response to academic misconduct. Sites such as the University of Michigan Library's "Plagiarism" page offer sample lessons and articles on plagiarism.

_____

_____

_____

Exercise 8: Writing

Complete the sentences to define an idea or invention from your current research or another class. Make sure they form a coherent paragraph.

Because _____, there has been growing interest in

_____ .

It is believed that _____, and _____

_____ .

However, researchers have not _____ .

This question is important since _____ .

For example, _____ .

If _____, _____ .

2.6 Summary of Punctuation

A. Table 2.2 summarizes the punctuation of equal and non-equal clauses. Pay close attention to the commas, periods, and semi-colons. In this table, *and* stands for any coordinating conjunction, *but* for any subordinating conjunction, and *however* for any sentence connector.

Table 2.2 Punctuation of Equal and Non-Equal Clauses			
Simple Sentences		(1a) IC.	(32) The United States is facing an obesity epidemic.
	Most common	(1b) IC. *However*, IC.	(33) Excess weight contributes to other health conditions, including cardio-vascular disease, diabetes, and asthma. **Additionally,** children who are obese tend to become obese adults.
	Less frequent	(1c) IC. [Subject], *however*, [rest of IC].	(34) Rare genetic conditions sometimes cause childhood obesity. **More typically, however,** nutrition and inactivity are the root of the problem.
	Infrequent	(1d) IC. IC, *however.*	(35) It is difficult for some people to find healthy food choices**, however.**
Compound Sentences (equal clauses)		(2a) IC, *and* IC.	(36) Determining the real cause of obesity is complicated, **and** little scientific data is available to support any single cause.
		(2b) IC; (*however,*) IC.	(37) Everyone can play a role in reducing obesity**; for example,** schools can provide nutritious lunches for children.
Complex Sentences (unequal clauses)		(3a) IC *because* DC.	(38) It is hard to eat fruit instead of chips or cookies **when** neighborhood stores carry little fresh produce.
		(3b) IC, DC.* * *non-finite*	(39) Junk food is digested quickly**, meaning** people feel hungry again sooner and need to consume more calories to feel full.
		(3c) DC, IC.	(40) **Although** numerous studies show that exercise reduces the risk of obesity**,** few schools provide the minimum recommended amount of physical education to their students.

Notes:

IC = independent clause; DC = dependent clause; *and* = any coordinating conjunction; *because* = any subordinating conjunction; *however* = any sentence connector.

Parentheses indicate an optional word. Complex sentences can be formed with relative clauses and noun clauses (Unit 3) as well as unequal clauses.

B. Although a comma usually separates two independent clauses joined with a coordinating conjunction (Sentence 36), the comma is not necessary with compounds that are not complete finite clauses.

> (41) Reporting the results of the experiment **and** discussing the
> implications of those results are usually separated in research papers
> **and** journal articles.

> (42) Input is necessary **but** not sufficient for language learning.

The subject of the second clause is often omitted if it is the same as the subject of the first clause.

> (43) Shifts toward democratization are not new of course **and** have been
> highlighted quite well.

C. Although a comma is not necessary in a sentence where the dependent clause follows the main clause (Sentence 38), many writers do use a comma with dependent clauses that express a strong contrast using subordinating conjunctions such as *although, even though,* or *while.*

> (44) There is no cure for MS [multiple sclerosis]**, although** a variety of
> drugs are used in an attempt to delay progression.

> (45) Engineers and future educators would learn calculus and physics
> concepts in the same way**, even though** they will use that information
> much differently in the future.

D. Notice that sentence connectors can move to different positions in the sentence, but some are frequently used in particular positions often. For example, *also* is far more common in the middle of the clause than at the start.

For more on the position of adverbs, see 6.3 in this book and Unit 3 (page 105) of *Academic Writing for Graduate Students,* 3rd edition.

> (46a) LESS COMMON: **Also**, some smartphones can
> display e-books.

> (46b) BETTER: Some smartphones can **also** display e-books.

Exercise 9: Editing

Read the sentences from an article by researchers at Texas A&M University on pollution ("Pollution haze," 2009) (1–5) and academic sentences from MICUSP (6–10). Identify the sentence type (1a, 2b, etc., from Table 2.2) and add the correct punctuation (commas, semi-colons, and periods).

_____ 1. "Blue haze" is a common occurrence in mountain ranges and forests around the world.

_____ 2. It is formed by natural emissions of chemicals but a recent study suggests human activities can worsen it.

_____ 3. This could even affect weather worldwide potentially causing climate problems.

_____ 4. The natural way of blue haze formation is rather inefficient.

_____ 5. A mix of natural and man-made chemicals speeds up the formation of these particles in the Earth's atmosphere and there they reflect sunlight back into space.

_____ 6. When you walk through a forest or even a large grassy area it's not uncommon to be able to smell the plants around you.

_____ 7. This dichotomy is expressed in terms of various other oppositions this separation however is fairly recent.

_____ 8. The issues call for employing the appropriate participation strategy for the situation therefore the following hypothesis is proposed.

_____ 9. These classes can help students meet their academic goals there are a few caveats to these positive findings however.

_____ 10. The government needs wise and honest laws thus it needs educated and virtuous lawmakers.

Exercise 10: Writing

Write two or three paragraphs explaining a concept from your field of study to people who are not experts in your discipline. Use a variety of clause combinations (equal clauses, unequal clauses, non-restrictive relative clauses, –ing clauses). In a different color, circle the connecting words (coordinating conjunctions, subordinating conjunctions, sentence connectors, linking prepositional phrases, and –ing clauses). Check the punctuation using Table 2.2. Finally, look for ways to develop the meaning of any simple sentences by adding clauses for elaboration, expansion, and extension (2.5).

_____

_____

_____

_____

_____

_____

2.7 Fragments and Run-Ons

A. Fragments and run-ons are not acceptable in most academic writing, although you might see and hear them in other places (email, newspapers, and spoken English).

B. **Run-on sentences** occur when two independent clauses are joined with a comma and no conjunction. Look for this error by counting the number of subjects and verbs in the sentences and then checking the punctuation. Run-on sentences can be corrected by adding a conjunction, changing the comma to a semi-colon, or adding a period after the first sentence.

> (47a) INCORRECT: Culture shock is not unusual**,** it happens to almost everyone who moves to a new place.

> (47b) CORRECT: Culture shock is not unusual**. It** happens to almost everyone who moves to a new place.

> (47c) CORRECT: Culture shock is not unusual**, for** it happens to almost everyone who moves to a new place.

> (47d) CORRECT: Culture shock is not unusual**;** it happens to almost everyone who moves to a new place.

C. Sentence connectors are sometimes mistaken for conjunctions, which also results in a run-on sentence (Sentence 48a). Sentence connectors link ideas between sentences, but they cannot connect clauses in an unequal relationship. You can use a semi-colon with a sentence connector, forming a compound sentence with equal clauses (Sentence 48b).

> (48a) INCORRECT: The first stage of culture shock is a positive experience, **however**, it gives way to an unpleasant feeling of disorientation.
>
> (48b) CORRECT: The first stage of culture shock is a positive experience; **however**, it gives way to an unpleasant feeling of disorientation.
>
> (48c) CORRECT: The first stage of culture shock is actually a positive experience. **However**, it gives way to an unpleasant feeling of disorientation.
>
> (48d) CORRECT: The first stage of culture shock is actually a positive experience, **but** it gives way to an unpleasant feeling of disorientation.

D. *Even* is an adverb, not a conjunction. Some writers use *even* when they mean *even if* or *even though* (2.5), but this produces another run-on sentence. *Even* is correctly used by itself to mean that something is surprising or unexpected.

> (49a) INCORRECT: **Even** everyone's experience of culture shock is different, there are four common stages.
>
> (49b) CORRECT: **Even though** everyone's experience of culture shock is different, there are four common stages.
>
> (49c) CORRECT: **Even** British students experience culture shock in the United States.

E. **Fragments** are sentences without a complete finite clause. This is generally inappropriate in academic writing, although sophisticated writers sometimes deliberately use fragments for effect. To correct a fragment, check that there is a subject and verb in the sentence. If the fragment is a dependent clause, consider adding an independent clause.

> (50a) INCORRECT: **Because** the new culture may seem familiar.
>
> (50b) CORRECT: **Because** the new culture may seem familiar, it is easy to miss important differences.

F. The object of a preposition cannot be any finite clause except for a **wh- word** noun clause (2.7). The object of a preposition can also be a noun phrase, an *–ing* non-finite clause, or a noun with an embedded clause (3.4). Some common prepositions that connect ideas and are often mistaken for conjunctions are: *because of, due to,* and *despite.*

(51a) INCORRECT: **Despite** they live in a country for many years, some people never fully assimilate.

(51b) CORRECT: **Despite living** in a country for many years, some people never fully assimilate.

(51c) CORRECT: **Despite the fact they have lived** in a country for many years, some people never fully assimilate.

(51d) CORRECT: **Despite how long they have lived** in a country, some people never fully assimilate.

G. Examples can be introduced with the prepositions *such as, for example,* and *for instance.* All three can be followed by one or more nouns or non-finite clauses. However, only *for example* and *for instance* can be used as sentence connectors. *Such as* cannot start a finite clause.

(52a) There are ways to ease the process of adaptation, **such as / for example / for instance** calling home, making new friends, and learning the local language.

(52b) There are many ways to ease the process of adaptation. **For example / For instance**, it is helpful to call home regularly.

(52c) INCORRECT: There are many ways to ease the process of adaptation. **Such as**, it is helpful to call home regularly.

Exercise 11: Clause Combination

Combine the clauses using the connectors in parentheses. Punctuate correctly.

1. Cell phones are growing in popularity. Land lines are becoming obsolete. (*because*)

    _____

    _____

2. Some companies ban Facebook during the work day. They allow employees to use it at lunchtime. (*although*)

    _____

    _____

3. Some experts say that TV is bad for children. Other researchers have found no harmful effects. (*however*)

    _____

    _____

4. There are many ways to balance online and face-to-face communication. You can turn off devices at mealtimes. *(such as)*

    _____

    _____

5. Many students believe they can multi-task efficiently. They are, in fact, less productive. *(even though)*

    _____

    _____

6. The Internet allows international students and their families to keep in touch. They live far away from each other. *(despite)*

    _____

    _____

Exercise 12: Editing

Find and correct the punctuation and clause combination errors, including fragments, run-ons, and –*ing* clauses in this definition of organically and locally grown food ("Organic and locally grown foods," 2009).

❶ Organic foods are produced without use antibiotics in animal feed, genetically engineered organisms, chemical preservatives, radiation, or artificial pesticides, herbicides, or fertilizers. ❷ Organic farming must also preserve the soil, and treat livestock humanely. ❸ Local food is less strictly defined, it may or may not be organic, but it is always purchased relatively near its place of production. ❹ Although, it was once seen as the concern of the eco-fringe. ❺ Organic and local foods have been changing the U.S., European, and global food markets rapidly over the last two decades.

❻ Organic and local foods are generally more expensive than similar foods grown by conventional means, consumers, therefore, are motivated to buy them because of they have certain values or conviction. ❼ Such as the concept that one's food should be produced by sustainable methods, or the assumption that organic foods are healthier.

❽ Critics of organic food argue that there is no scientific evidence that most organics are healthier to eat. ❾ But, advocates of organic and local foods hope for several benefits. ❿ First, there is the wish to be part of an agricultural system that cares for the long-term wellbeing of the natural world rather than exploit it for short-term profit. ⓫ Conventional large-scale agriculture is one of the most polluting industries and is causing rapid loss of soil in many parts of the world; organic agriculture causes less pollution, slows soil loss, and increases local biodiversity. ⓬ Second, organic and local-food advocates hope to reinforce local communities and economies, which funneling consumer dollars to small farmers, many of which struggle to survive financially. ⓭ Third, many shoppers seeking fresher foods choose locally grown foods with less transit time to market. ⓮ Moreover, there is some scientific evidence that eating organic foods may, in fact, be healthier; because such foods contain fewer hazardous chemicals (such as pesticide residues) and more nutrients.

Grammar in Your Discipline

A. Look through an article or book in your academic discipline and find examples of:

   1. equal and unequal clauses

   2. conjunctions and sentence connectors

   3. non-restrictive relative clauses

   4. reduced non-restrictive relative clauses

B. Look again at your text and answer these questions.

   1. Which are more common: unreduced or reduced relative clauses?

   _____

   2. Do you see any *–ing* clauses (reduced non-restrictive relative clauses) frequently? How are they used? _____

C. Share your findings with a small group of writers from other disciplines. Do you notice any similarities or differences?

D. Write an extended definition of a term from your field of study that is unfamiliar to people outside your discipline. Combine clauses using the techniques in the unit to help you explain the idea fully.

> For more information and examples of extended definitions, see Unit 2 of *Academic Writing for Graduate Students,* 3rd edition.

Embedded, Noun, and Complement Clauses

Unit 2 described ways of combining independent and dependent clauses. Unit 3 considers different techniques for combining clauses in which one clause becomes part of, or embedded in, another clause. Restrictive relative clauses, for example, are embedded in a noun phrase; noun clauses typically function as the complement of a reporting verb, and complement clauses are embedded in structures such as *it is important for you to study this unit.*

UNIT 3 Preview Test

Correct the errors in this report about the English Language Proficiency Assessment that is administered to school children who speak English as a second language ("English Proficiency," 2011).

❶ The nationally mandated language proficiency test given to students that second language is English causes psychological stress for children, who can least afford it, a new study shows. ❷ Without some major overhaul, the English Language Proficiency Assessment is expected that it will negatively impact the academic success of the country's more than five million English Language Learners, who defined as those who speak another language.

❸ "The test is supposed to measure how well a school teaches English, but the students feel it measures their own abilities and that they're a good person," says Paula Winke, assistant professor of Second Language Studies at Michigan State University. ❹ So students often don't understand why is the test so difficult. ❺ They think, 'Why am I such a failure?'"

Grammar Awareness: The Introduction

Read this paragraph from the introduction to a student's paper for a political science course (included in MICUSP) about the Truth and Reconciliation Commission, which was created when South Africa gave full rights to black citizens.

The Truth and Reconciliation Commission (TRC), constitutionally ❶ <u>mandated</u> by the 1995 Promotion of National Unity and Reconciliation Act, attempted to use the revelation of truth about the injustices ❷ <u>that occurred</u> during the apartheid[1] regime in order to promote national healing. Beginning in 1996, it functioned under ❸ <u>the belief that</u> the best way to heal past wounds from apartheid was uncovering truth about wrongs ❹ <u>inflicted</u> against other citizens. The committee consisted of three bodies: the Human Rights Violations Committee, ❺ <u>which</u> investigated apartheid-era human rights violations, the Reparation and Rehabilitation Committee, ❻ <u>which</u> worked to restore victims' dignity, and the Amnesty Committee, ❼ <u>which</u> had the power to grant amnesty to perpetrators (black or white) ❽ <u>based</u> upon full disclosure of actions and proof of political purposes. The effectiveness of the TRC is highly debated by both citizens and scholars. While it did reveal the truth about many of the disappearances and murders ❾ <u>which</u> had plagued individual families, few high-ranking apartheid era officials applied for amnesty, and the court of South Africa has failed to prosecute those ❿ <u>that</u> did not apply, effectively ⓫ <u>delegitimizing</u> the work of the court. However, more importantly, most ⓬ <u>agree that</u> the commission failed to address the violations of social and economic rights ⓭ <u>perpetrated</u> by the apartheid regime, opting to focus mainly on more visual violations of civil and political rights. But what are the actual reasons for this failure, and how has it affected the future of socio-economic rights in South Africa?

1. The beginnings of 13 clauses are underlined in the text. Categorize them according to any system that is meaningful to you, and explain your categories to a partner. Then answer the questions.

2. What is the difference in function between Clauses 2 and 5?

3. What is the difference in structure between Clauses 8 and 9?

4. What are the differences between Clauses 2, 3, and 12?

---

[1] Apartheid was the South African government's policy of separating whites and non-whites. Only white South Africans could vote and serve in the government from 1948 until 1994.

3.1 Embedded Clauses (Restrictive Relative Clauses)

A. A **restrictive relative clause** restricts the meaning of a noun phrase. The relative clause becomes part of the main clause because it is **embedded** in one of the noun phrases (1.2). Restrictive relative clauses are sometimes called identifying or defining clauses because, unlike non-restrictive clauses, they specify the meaning of the noun they modify.

B. The difference between restrictive and non-restrictive **relative clauses** is important and can change the meaning of a sentence. Because they are part of the noun phrase, embedded clauses are not separated with commas, unlike non-restrictive relative clauses.

> (1a) The students**, who had been nervous about questioning the
> adults,** were very excited about the results of their interviews. [non-
> restrictive relative clause, elaborating]

> (1b) The students **who had been nervous about questioning the
> adults** were very excited about the results of their interviews. [restrictive
> relative clause, embedded]

In Sentence 1a, all the students were excited, and the writer adds that they all had been nervous. The logical relationship between the clauses is elaboration (2.5). In Sentence 1b, only the students who had been nervous were excited; the others (who had not been nervous) presumably were bored. In other words, the relative clause is embedded in the noun phrase *the students who . . .* , and it tells us *which* students were excited, rather than extending the meaning of the entire main clause.

C. Table 3.1 summarizes the relative pronouns available for both types of relative clauses.[2]

Table 3.1 Relative Pronouns			
	Human Referent	**Non-Human Referent**	**Possessive**
Restrictive/Embedded	who, whom, that	which, that	whose
Non-Restrictive (with commas)	who, whom	which	whose

D. The **relative pronoun** *whom* is fairly rare, especially in scientific and technical fields, and its use overall appears to be declining slowly, according to corpus data. Traditionally, *whom* is used for human referents when the pronoun is a complement slot in the relative clause.

> (2a) They could choose **whom to work with**.

In sentences such as Sentence 2a, the preposition can also be moved in front of the pronoun (Sentence 2b).

> (2b) They could choose **with whom to work**.

This is a very formal style of writing, and although traditional grammar books disapprove of prepositions at the end of clauses and sentences (Sentence 2a), the practice is very common in all forms of English.

---

[2] Note that both *which* and *that* are grammatically correct in embedded (restrictive) relative clauses. However, some style guides (notably the *Chicago Manual of Style*) and many instructors insist on *that* for restrictive clauses.

Exercise 1: Grammar Analysis

Identify the type of relative clause. Write R for restrictive or NR for non-restrictive. Circle the referent (the noun, phrase, or clause to which the relative clause is attached).

_____ 1. Approximately 41.3 million Hispanics live in the United States, **constituting almost half of the population in California, Texas, and New Mexico.**

_____ 2. Many Hispanic citizens will be academically hindered in the future by the academic instruction **that they missed** while struggling to learn enough English.

_____ 3. The United States was based upon the model of a melting pot **in which all people harmoniously come together to form one united nation.**

_____ 4. Countries such as Switzerland and Belgium have multiple *official* languages, **which would imply an even greater public recognition and integration.**

_____ 5. Recognizing Spanish as a national language would ease the transition into English-only classrooms, thus raising the rate of **students who become truly proficient in both English and Spanish.**

Exercise 2: Writing Definitions

Choose four key terms from your field of study or research, and write a one-sentence definition for each.

- (A/an) _____ is a _____ that _____
            term   *category of thing*   *distinguishing features*

- (A/an) _____ who/that _____ is called a _____.
            category   *distinguishing features*   *name*

- (A/an) _____ is/does _____, meaning _____.
            term   *function/description*   *explanation*

- (A/an) _____ is a _____ whose _____.
            term   *category*   *description of component*

> For more examples of one-sentence definitions, please refer to Unit 2 (pages 71–74) of *Academic Writing for Graduate Students*, 3rd edition.

3.2 Reduced Embedded Clauses

A. Finite (full) relative clauses are often **reduced** to non-finite (*–ed* or *–ing*) clauses or prepositional phrases in academic writing, leading to a more concise but denser style. Reduction also allows the writer to make noun phrases more specific without distracting the reader with additional verbs. When reducing relative clauses, be sure to delete the relative pronoun and either delete or change the verb. These strategies may be used to reduce relative clauses:

1. *be* + **prepositional phrase**

(3) Protected values are firmly held ethical beliefs ~~which are~~ **about** one's duties and rights as a human being.

(4) Milgram conducted similar experiments ~~which were~~ **on** different groups of people.

2. passive

(5) Scaffolding refers to guidance ~~which is~~ **provided** by adults or peers.

(6) The Filipino that Filipinos use in day-to-day interactions is different than the Filipino ~~which is~~ **found** in textbooks and used in classrooms.

(7) The basic quantum computation scheme ~~which is/has been~~ **envisioned** here requires the ability to separate and shuttle ions.

3. progressive verb tenses

(8) The work of educational researchers ~~who are~~ **looking** at foreign language learning takes into account many different factors.

4. *be* + *–able* **adjective**

(9) Iron oxide is a fragile and brittle compound ~~which is~~ **not suitable** for use as reinforcement.

(10) Experienced employees ~~who are~~ **capable** of high production levels will balk at the compensation system changes.

5. *have* **(as a main verb)** → *with*

(11) This captures the dynamics of many infectious diseases ~~which have~~ *with* just a few interactions.

(12) Many of its citizens live in inner-city neighborhoods ~~that have~~ *with* high levels of crime.

6. many linking verbs, or verbs that describe facts → non-finite –*ing* clauses

attempting
(13) This paper proposes a line of work ~~which attempts~~ to incorporate the effects of emotion on cognition.

7. non-finite (*to*) clauses

(14) Another weakness ~~which is~~ **to be discussed** is the small sample size used for this project.

(15) Its truth or correctness would explain the intuitive appeal of the other ideas ~~which are~~ **to be** discussed.

B. One piece of information that is lost in a reduced clause is **tense**. Since most academic writing is in the present simple tense, this is not usually a problem, but sometimes the full clause is needed for clarity. However, clauses with **modal verbs** (e.g., *may, might, can, could*) cannot be reduced without losing the meaning of the modal verb (5.2–5.4).

(16a) This is a problem **that might be** solved by technology

(16b) This is a problem **solved** by technology.

Sometimes, you can change the modal verb to an adverb with a similar meaning.

(16c) This is a problem **potentially solved** by technology.

> For more practice with reducing clauses, refer to *Academic Writing for Graduate Students,* 3rd edition (pages 391–394), from which this description is adapted.

Exercise 3: Sentence Combination

Combine these sentences from a report about research at the University of Rochester on the star system known as the Big Dipper ("Star found," 2009). Use both embedded and non-restrictive relative clauses as needed and reduce them where possible.

Example: In ancient times, people thought that one of the stars in the Big Dipper was actually two stars. These people had exceptional eyesight.

In ancient times, people with exceptional eyesight thought that one of the stars in the Big Dipper was actually two stars.

1. The two stars were the first binary stars ever known. They are called Alcor and Mizar.

_____

_____

2. Modern telescopes have since found that Mizar is itself a pair of binaries. This reveals that there are actually four stars orbiting each other.

_____

_____

3. Alcor has been sometimes considered a fifth member of the system. It orbits far away from the Mizar quadruplet.

_____

_____

4. Now, an astronomer has made the surprise discovery that Alcor is also actually two stars. The astronomer is at the University of Rochester.

_____

_____

5. "Instead of finding a planet, we found a star. The planet orbits Alcor."

_____

_____

6. Another group of scientists used the Multiple Mirror Telescope in Arizona. This has a secondary mirror. The mirror is capable of flexing slightly to compensate for the twinkling. The Earth's atmosphere normally imparts this twinkling to starlight.

_____

_____

_____

Exercise 4: Sentence Completion

Complete each sentence by adding an embedded clause (full or reduced).

1. Businesses use Internet advertising to target customers. _____

   _____

2. Cell phone companies are competing to produce new batteries. _____

   _____

3. Biomedical researchers hope to discover cures for diseases. _____

   _____

4. Some professors have experimented with online discussion boards. _____

   _____

5. Experts recommend that children engage in physical activity every day at school. _____

   _____

3.3 Noun Clauses

A. **Noun clauses** are dependent clauses that are usually complements of reporting or linking verbs (1.6., 1.7), but they can also complement nouns or adjectives (3.4). Less commonly, noun clauses can stand as the subject of a clause. In academic writing, noun clauses are often used to report what other people think or have said, such as when introducing a paraphrase, summary, or quotation.

B. There are three types of noun clauses. Each is formed in a different way.

1. When the noun clause is a statement, use *that* as the subordinator. You can delete *that*, but most academic writers keep it.

   (17) Researchers have found **(that) bacteria are present**.

2. When the noun clause is formed from a yes/no question, use *if* or *whether* as the subordinator. There is no difference in meaning between *if* and *whether*, but *if* is used less frequently in academic writing than in conversation (Biber et al., 1999, p. 691). Use statement word order, not inverted question word order.

   (18) Researchers wonder **if/whether bacteria are present**.

3. When the noun clause is formed from a *wh-* question, use the *wh-* word as the subordinator. Use statement word order.

(19) Researchers ask **where bacteria are present**.

The second two types are called indirect questions in *Academic Writing for Graduate Students* (see pages 133–135) and some other grammar books because they are formed from questions but written as statements.

C. Some reporting verbs require certain types of noun clauses. For example, *wonder* can be followed by *if, whether*, or any *wh-* word clause, but it cannot be followed by a *that* clause. *Argue* is usually followed by a *that* clause but is almost never followed by any other type of noun clause because writers argue about statements of opinion. *Realize* takes *that* and *what* clauses but no other *wh-* words, *if,* or *whether*. To check the possible noun clauses with any verb, consult a good dictionary or online corpus (Unit 7).

D. Any noun clause can serve as the subject of a clause, but this is an unusual structure.

(20) **That bacteria are present** is surprising.

E. An alternative to using a noun clause is using a direct quotation. However, research suggests that quoting is far less common than paraphrasing and summarizing in most academic fields, and it is almost non-existent in the sciences and engineering (Hyland, 2000, p. 26). When quotations are used, writers can choose whether or not to include a clause with a reporting verb; the connecting word *that* is also optional. Notice that a comma is not used before or after *that* (Sentence 22).

(21) Serketich and Dumas (1996) **reported,** "Age had a significant, positive correlation with effect size."

(22) Brennan (1982) **reported that** "adolescence seems to be the time of life when loneliness first emerges as an intense recognizable phenomenon" (p. 269).

(23) **According to Losyukov,** "these are most sincere fears." [No reporting verb; the prepositional phrase *according to* . . . introduces the quotation.]

Exercise 5: Sentence Revision

Read these sentences from an article about research conducted at the University of California–Berkeley on text messaging ("Text therapy," 2012). Rewrite each sentence using the subject in parentheses, a reporting verb, and a noun clause. Since the sentences are direct quotations from the article, you should paraphrase your revisions.

> For a detailed discussion of paraphrasing and plagiarism, see Unit 5 (pages 196–198) of *Academic Writing for Graduate Students*, 3rd edition.

Example: Receiving text messages can make people feel less isolated. *(article)*

The article reports that text messages can reduce isolation.

1. My patients report feeling more connected and cared for when they receive text messages. *(Professor Adrian Aguilera)*

   _____

   _____

2. When I was in a difficult situation and I received a message, I felt much better. *(a female patient in Aguilera's cognitive behavior therapy group)*

   _____

   _____

3. African American and Latino mobile phone owners send and receive more text messages than Caucasians do. *(the Pew Research Center)*

   _____

   _____

4. Who are the most active senders and receivers of text messages? *(the study)*

   _____

   _____

5. Can I send text messages to remind patients to practice the skills covered in therapy sessions? *(Aguilera)*

   _____

   _____

6. About 75 percent of the patients asked to continue receiving the messages. *(researchers)*

   _____

   _____

Exercise 6: Writing

Choose an article that you have recently read. Write a summary using at least four of these sentence starters.

The article reports	*The author(s) found*	*Previous research has suggested*
The author(s) wonder	*The study asked*	*He/She/They conclude(s)*
The problem is	*According to the article*	*The paper implies*

3.4 Complement Noun Clauses

A. Sometimes, a noun clause can be embedded in a noun phrase or be used after an adjective. In these cases, it can be called a **complement clause** because it complements (i.e., completes) the meaning of the noun or adjective. The most common nouns that are complemented by noun clauses are *claim, argument,* and *fact.*

(24) **The claim that** retention works is not supported.

(25) **The fact that** the earliest examples of cotton fabric were found in a river valley is significant.

In Sentence 24, the writer implies that some people have claimed that retention (keeping students back in the same grade for a second year) works. By embedding the clause in a noun phrase, the writer is able to raise the idea that retention works and also disagree with it in one sentence. In Sentence 25, the noun clause is presented as a fact. This choice carries more interpersonal meaning; the writer presents facts in Sentence 24 rather than a debate in Sentence 25 (6.6).

B. Other nouns followed by embedded *that* clauses include: *notion, belief, assumption, view, way, hypothesis, conclusion, chance, possibility, probability, proof, principle, point,* and *evidence.*

C. Embedded noun clauses can be used in contexts where a *that* noun clause would not usually be grammatical, such as after a preposition (3.6).

(26) All papers seemed to be logical and well-organized, partly **due to the fact that** all scientific papers follow a similar format.

(27) It is possible that other factors are causing the anthropologists' poor health outcomes, **such as the fact that** they are overworking themselves.

D. Some nouns can be complemented by an embedded *wh-* word clause, such as *the reason why, the point where, the place where,* and *the time/moment/day when.*

> (28) **The reason why** people care so much about reputation is that they continuously seek approval and respect.
>
> (29a) The zone of proximal development is the **place where** teaching takes place.
>
> (29b) The zone of proximal development is the **place in which** teaching occurs.

The embedded clause in Sentence 29a is very similar to the other type of embedded clause, a restrictive relative clause. In fact, it can be replaced by a clause starting with a preposition + relative pronoun (Sentence 29b).

E. However, it is important to distinguish embedded *that* clauses from restrictive relative clauses. In a relative clause, the **subordinator** (*that, which,* or *who*) is the subject or object (agent, goal, or recipient) in the dependent clause; in a noun clause, the subordinator (usually *that*) only introduces the **subordinate clause.**

> (30) This is supported **by the fact that** all these cases occur in the tropics and subtropical regions. [noun clause: *it is a fact that all these cases occur in these regions*]
>
> (31) This is supported by the fact **that** we described earlier. [relative clause: *that* means *fact*, the fact was described earlier]

F. Noun clauses can also complement many adjectives describing feelings or opinions.

> (32) People continue to be **surprised that** African countries have such low growth rates.
>
> (33) It is not **surprising that** these results were so hard to find.
>
> (34) It is truly **unfortunate that** women continue to be subjected to sexism.
>
> (35) It is **not clear why** Aristotle does not make the stronger claim.

Exercise 7: Sentence Writing

Think of an idea in your field of study or research. Complete each definition sentence with a noun clause, embedded noun clause, or relative clause.

1. A/an _____ is a/an _____ that _____

   _____.

2. A/an _____ is especially useful/important due to the _____

   that _____.

3. The fact that _____ means

   _____.

4. It is (not) clear that/why _____.

5. The claim that _____ is likely/unlikely to

   be true because _____.

6. Some people may be surprised that _____.

7. The reason why _____ is

   _____.

3.5 *To* Non-Finite Clauses and Subjunctive Clauses

A. Non-finite clauses formed with *to* plus the base form of the verb (often called the infinitive form) have several functions. According to Biber et al.'s (1999) corpus analysis, the use of *to* non-finite clauses rather than *that* finite clauses is one way that academic writing differs from everyday English.

1. They complement certain reporting verbs in place of a (finite) noun clause (1.6).
2. They can serve as subjects, although *-ing* clauses are more common (2.4).
3. They often function as the complements of adjectives, which will be discussed in this section.

B. A *to* non-finite clause can complement a wide range of adjectives in a linking verb clause. Some of the most frequent adjectives have the meanings of possibility (*likely, unlikely*), ability (*able, unable, willing, unwilling*), and difficulty (*hard, easy, difficult*).

(36) Depression is twice as **likely to occur** in women as in men.

(37) Most people are **unwilling to take** long-term tests.

A subject for the non-finite verb can be introduced with *for*.

(38) The money needed to supply widespread education is **difficult for a poor country to provide.** [the money is not difficult; providing the money is difficult]

C. Another common sentence structure is *it is* + adjective + *to* clause. The adjectives used indicate necessity (*important, necessary, essential, crucial, critical*), difficulty (*difficult, possible, impossible, easy, hard*), and evaluation (*interesting, reasonable, useful, tempting, appropriate, safe, helpful, good, better, best, valuable, sufficient*).

(39) **It is important to provide** a more comprehensive answer to what successful species conservation means.

(40) Under such circumstances **it is appropriate to extend** some national rights over ocean resources

D. An alternative clause combination exists with adjectives that express necessity, urgency, or request. In these cases, a *that* noun clause may be used with the verb in the **subjunctive form**. The subjunctive is the base form of the verb without *to*. A subjunctive verb does not agree with its subject (*that he go*). For negative verbs, insert *not* before the verb (Sentence 44). The subjunctive is also used after verbs with similar meanings (*demand, ask, urge, recommend*). Subjunctive clauses are rare now even in formal contexts and can easily be avoided with a *to* complement clause.

(41) It is essential that the government **recognize** the expanded core curriculum as a necessary element of the educational experience of students who are visually impaired.

(42) This law requires that almost every third to eighth grader **be tested** in reading, mathematics, and science every year.

(43) He goes on to demand that this relation **be** an authentic one.

(44) It is important that immigration policy **not be confused** with immigrant policy.

According to the *Corpus of Historical American English*, use of the subjunctive began to decline after the 1970s. When the subjunctive is used, data from the *Corpus of Contemporary American English* show that it is more frequent in the humanities, philosophy, law, and political science than in the sciences and social sciences.

Exercise 8: Sentence Writing

Choose a problem in your field, university, or school, and write sentences using *to* clauses or the subjunctive form as appropriate. Use at least five of these opening clauses.

1. _____ is/are difficult to _____

2. People are likely/unlikely _____

3. It is important _____

4. Experts urge that _____

5. We should demand that _____

6. It is crucial _____

7. It is necessary _____

8. It is essential _____

9. I ask that _____

10. Researchers recommend _____

3.6 Common Problems

A. Many writers find the punctuation of relative clauses difficult. Commas separate non-restrictive clauses from the main clause, but they are not used with restrictive clauses because these clauses are embedded in a noun phrase. Proficient speakers of English should be able to hear a change in pitch and/or a pause when they say a sentence with a non-restrictive clause.

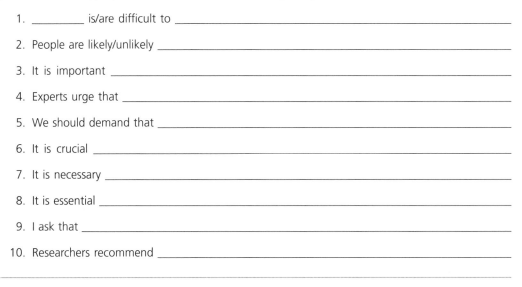

(45) Unlike consumer **debts**, // which are paid regularly and can be terminated or initiated, // credit card debt and other debt do not have temporal constraints.

There is a slight rise in intonation on the referent noun *(debts)*, followed by a short pause; the relative clause is spoken at a slightly lower pitch and is also followed by a short pause before the speaker resumes the main clause at a normal pitch. When this technique is not possible, ask whether the relative clause refers to *all* of the noun phrase (non-restrictive) or just *some* of the noun phrase (embedded).

(46) There are two genes involved in eye color mutations, **which are located on chromosome II.**

In Sentence 46, there are only two genes, and they are both located on chromosome II, so the clause is non-restrictive and the comma is correct. Without the comma, the clause would be embedded, and the sentence would mean that two of the genes involved in eye color mutations are located on chromosome II, but other genes with this function are located on other chromosomes.

B. The relative pronoun *that* cannot be used in non-restrictive relative clauses.

> (47a) INCORRECT: This is distinguished from the hybrids that are currently being marketed, **that** do not use any electricity from the grid.
>
> (47b) CORRECT: This is distinguished from hybrids that are currently being marketed, **which** do not use any electricity from the grid.

C. Remember that noun clauses only need one subordinator.

> (48a): INCORRECT: The consumer may not even know **that why** they are taking the drug at all.
>
> (48b) CORRECT: The consumer may not even know **why** they are taking the drug at all.

D. Only use a question mark if the independent clause is a question, even if the noun clause looks like a question.

> (49a) INCORRECT: **Researchers wondered** which bacteria were present**?**
>
> (49b) CORRECT: **Has anyone asked** which bacteria were present**?**
>
> (49c) CORRECT: **Researchers wondered** which bacteria were present**.**

E. Only *wh-* and *whether* noun clauses can be the complement of a preposition (not *that* or *if* clauses).

> (50a) INCORRECT: The findings received attention **because of that** they were reported in *Nature*.
>
> (50b) CORRECT: The findings received attention **because of where** they were reported.

F. Non-native speakers should be especially careful with complement *to* non-finite clauses after adjectives of difficulty.

> (51a) INCORRECT: Workers **are easy to obtain** new deadlines. [This incorrectly means that the workers are easy, not obtaining new deadlines.]
>
> (51b) CORRECT: **Obtaining a new deadline** is easy for workers to do.
>
> (51c) CORRECT: **It is easy for workers to obtain** new deadlines.
> CORRECT: Workers can easily obtain new deadlines.

G. It is common to use an embedded clause (full or reduced) after *there is /are*. However, be careful not to use a finite verb.

(52a) INCORRECT: There are other reasons **support** this theory.

(52b) CORRECT: There are other reasons **which support** this theory.

(52c) CORRECT: There are other reasons **supporting** this theory.

In Sentence 52a, the subject is *there,* and the finite verb is *are,* so *reasons* is the complement and therefore cannot also be the subject of the finite verb *support.* However, in Sentence 52b, *support* is embedded in a clause which modifies the noun *reasons* (the reasons for what?). Sentence 52c is a reduced version of this sentence.

Exercise 9: Editing

Read the sentences adapted from a sociology research paper and correct the embedded, noun, and complement clauses (including punctuation).

1. The survey asked that an unhappy marriage is preferable to divorce.

2. This is especially true for western China which is less developed.

3. I investigated how do socioeconomic factors affect attitudes toward marriage.

4. It is crucial investigating gender disparities in attitudes toward unhappy marriages.

5. There are three types of independent variables are used for this study.

6. A set of ideational variables which indicating modernity factors are included.

7. The results indicate, that women are more likely to prefer divorce to an unhappy marriage.

8. This study is a critical step to further understand how people's family values are associated with demographic factors.

9. These variables are a test of if more modern respondents are more likely to prefer divorce.

10. Due to that minority ethnic groups dominate about 9% of the total population in China, Gansu is very representative.

Exercise 10: Writing

Identify a claim, theory, or idea in your field of study that you strongly agree or disagree with. Write a paragraph summarizing the claim and a second paragraph with your response and opinion. Try to use all the embedded clauses (restrictive relative clauses, noun clauses, and complement clauses). Then read your paper aloud to a partner. Ask each other questions about the content. If your partner does not understand a word or idea in your writing, consider adding a clause to explain it better. Finally, edit your writing for common errors and other problems with these clauses. Refer to Unit 2 if you need to review run-ons, fragments, and other common problems with clause combination.

Grammar in Your Discipline

A. Look through an article or book in your academic discipline and find examples of:

1. embedded (restrictive relative) clauses

2. reduced relative clauses

3. noun clauses using *that, wh-* words, or *if / whether*

4. subjunctive noun clauses (these might be hard to find!)

5. complement clauses

B. Look again at your texts, and answer these questions.

1. Which are more common: full, reduced, or embedded clauses?

   _____

2. Do writers in your field seem to prefer finite or non-finite complement clauses, or do they use both about equally?

   _____

3. Do writers in your field use direct questions or indirect questions (noun clauses)?

   _____

C. Share your findings with a small group of writers from other disciplines. Do you notice any similarities or differences? _____

D. Choose an article you read recently in your field of study. Imagine it is an author's manuscript that has been submitted to a journal but not yet published. The editor has asked you to review the article and recommend whether to publish it. You can make four recommendations:

1. accept and publish (explain why)

2. accept with minor revisions (explain what revisions should be made)

3. revise and submit (help the author to revise it; the editors will then decide whether to publish it)

4. reject (explain why)

> For advice on writing article critiques, see Unit 6 of *Academic Writing for Graduate Students*, 3rd edition. See *Navigating Academia* (Swales & Feak, 2011) for tips on writing letters to journal editors.

Use a variety of clause combination and embedding techniques from this unit and Unit 2. Edit for clause structure and punctuation.

UNIT

4

Verb Forms

The verb is the central slot in the English clause. It controls the grammatical structure and meaning of the clause. Verbs can be modified in four ways (Biber et al., 1999, p. 452).

1. **Time** (When did the action happen?): past or present?

2. **Aspect** (Is the action finished or ongoing?): simple, perfect, progressive (continuous), or perfect progressive (continuous)

3. **Voice** (Is the agent the subject of the verb?): active or passive

4. **Modality** (What is the writer's stance toward the action?): adding a modal verb (e.g., *will, can, may, should*)

This unit focuses on verb tense, defined as *time + aspect*—for example, present simple or past perfect. Voice is also discussed because every tense has active and passive forms, giving 16 possible combinations (4.1). Fortunately, only a small number of tenses are frequent in academic writing. Unit 2 describes how many writers use the most frequent tenses most of the time. However, there are many cases where writers do something different because of personal preference, style, or information structure. To help you understand how writers use verb tenses, read widely in your field and look closely at the verbs. Pay special attention to unusual choices, and ask yourself why the writer chose that tense. The fourth way to modify a verb— modality—is introduced in Unit 6.

UNIT 4 Preview Test
Choose a verb tense to complete these sentences. Discuss your choices.

1. Takahashi et al. _____ that most reported oral non-Hodgkin's lymphomas were B-cell lymphomas.
   a. note   b. are noting   c. have noted   d. noted

2. Research _____ few insights into why different attitudes exist.
   a. provides   b. is providing   c. has provided   d. provided

3. Currently, very few studies _____ this issue (Mu, Kurozawa, & Wang, 2006).
   a. examine   b. are examining   c. have examined   d. examined

4. Today professors _____ more advanced technology such as PowerPoint and Blackboard to deliver course information (Bork, 2000; Mines, 2000).
   a. use   b. are using   c. have used   d. used

5. These multiple purposes and audiences _____ textbooks to their discipline.
   a. link   b. are linking   c. have linked   d. linked

6. Their results _____ that at about -33° C surface melting starts.
   a. indicate   b. are indicating   c. have indicated   d. indicated

63

Grammar Awareness: Literature Review

Read the excerpt from a paper for a sociology class (included in MICUSP) and complete the tasks on page 65.

In a 1975 volume of the *American Sociological Review*, Treiman and Terrell (1975) **reflect** that the 1970s could be characterized as the time when research on women **began** in earnest in the academic community. They **comment**, "Just a few years ago, women **were excluded** from stratification studies on the grounds that their experiences **were** too complicated for analysis" (174). Thirty years later, research on women—and particularly women and work—**has made** considerable progress both in its quality and inclusion in mainstream sociological journals. While the research agenda on women in work **is** by no means exhausted, it **is** certainly substantial enough to warrant a retrospective of the field and propose some areas where the field **has** room for greater theorizing and empirical research.

In 1975, there **was** little empirical work yet completed that **addressed** the gendered process of status attainment in the workplace (Treiman & Terrell, 1975). The primary interest of status attainment research at this time **was related** to earnings differences between men and women. Treiman and Terrell (1975), for example, **attempted** to unpack the relationship between gender and earnings by comparing earnings of husbands and wives. They **found** that after controlling for hours worked, wives still **earn** less than half of what their husbands earn. The methodological problems with comparing wives' earnings to husbands' wages **seem** obvious to researchers today, but at the time this article **was written**, there **was** a burgeoning interest in comparing husband and wives' participation and success in the occupational sphere. Some **believed** increased wage earnings for women **would threaten** the stability of the family, and research that investigated the effect of women's employment and earnings on divorce rates **began** to emerge (Oppenheimer, 1977; Hannan, Tuma, & Groeneveld, 1978; Huber and Spitze, 1980).

Treiman and Terrell (1975) also **showed** that single women **earn** more than married women, another area of increasing interest as women **entered** the workforce. While this study's design and methodology **seem** simplistic and problematic given the research progress made in the sub-field of women in work over the past thirty years, it **does signal** a new interest in earnings and status inequality issues within the academy during the 1970s. This early study **is** also noteworthy for its data disaggregation between white and non-white women. One of the criticisms of research on women and work as well as the first wave of U.S. feminism **is** its lack of attention to gender differences across race. The Treiman and Terrell study **points** to sociologists' understanding of potential interaction effects between race and gender as early as the 1970s, and subsequent sociological research **has continued** to attend to this issue (Burstein, 1979; Greenman, forthcoming).

1. Which verb tenses do you see in this excerpt from a graduate student's literature review?

   _____

2. Mark three examples of a shift, or change, in verb tense or aspect within a paragraph. Why do you think the writer made those choices? Do you agree with them?

   _____

3. Look closely at the examples of the present perfect. How is this tense used?

   _____

4. What do you notice about verb tenses in noun clauses? Are they related to the tense of the main clause or independent?

   _____

5. Are there any verb tenses/aspects that you do *not* see in this excerpt? Are you surprised by their absence?

   _____

4.1 Summary of Verb Tenses

A. Table 4.1 shows the forms of the English tenses for a regular verb (*explain*) and an irregular verb (*find*).

Table 4.1 Summary of Verb Forms				
	Simple	**Perfect**	**Progressive**	**Perfect Progressive**
Present **Active**	(4.2) He explains She finds	(4.3) He has explained She has found	(4.4) He is explaining She is finding	(4.5) He has been explaining She has been finding
Passive	It is explained It is found	It has been explained It has been found	It is being explained It is being found	It has been being explained It has been being found
Past **Active**	(4.2) He explained She found	(4.5) He had explained She had found	(4.4) He was explaining She was finding	(4.5) He had been explaining She had been finding
Passive	It was explained It was found	It had been explained It had been found	It was being explained It was being found	It had been being explained It has been being found

The three tenses (in active and passive voice) in shaded boxes account for the majority of tensed verb phrases[1] in academic writing: the present simple (about 70 percent of tensed verbs); the past simple (around 23 percent); and the present perfect (about 5 percent of verbs). The other tenses occur extremely rarely: that is, you can choose from these three tenses for more than 98 percent of verbs that need tense (Biber et al., 1999, pp. 456–461).

B. Certain types of verbs prefer certain tenses. For example, linking verbs are predominantly used in the simple tenses (present simple and past simple) but very rarely in progressive tenses. Reporting verbs are common in both simple and perfect tenses, but again not progressive ones. Only action verbs are used with any frequency in progressive tenses, but this type of meaning (something that is happening right now) is not often useful in academic writing.

C. The choice of tense affects all three levels of meaning (1.8). The tense can tell the reader when an event happened or started and whether it is completed or ongoing (experiential meaning); it can indicate whether the writer considers the event or state to be relevant or true today (interpersonal meaning); and it can reorganize information through the choice of passive voice (textual meaning).

---

[1] Non-tensed verb phrases include clauses with modal verbs and non-finite clauses.

4.2 Present and Past Simple Tenses

A. The present simple tense is the basic tense of academic writing. Choose this unless there is a good reason to use another tense. Specifically, the present simple is used:

1. to "frame" a paper. In an introduction, the present simple tense describes what is *already known* about the topic (Sentence 1); in a conclusion, the tense says what is *now known* about the topic and what further research *is still needed* (Sentence 2).

   (1) Scholars **share** a common argument that engineering **is** the most male dominated of all professions.

   (2) Timing of college enrollment **is** associated with a number of variables.

2. to make general statements, conclusions, or interpretations about previous research or data, again focusing on what is known *now*.

   (3) Graduate school **is** regarded as crucial for starting an engineering career because failure at this stage effectively **closes** the door to professional engineering careers, and later career trajectory change **is** more difficult the longer it **is** delayed.

3. to cite a previous study or finding without mentioning the researcher in the sentence (Swales & Feak, 2012, p. 344).

   (4) Children **ingest** roughly 50–200 mg soil/day [2,3].

   (5) Job satisfaction **is** the most extensively studied variable in organizational behavior research (Spector, 1997).

4. to introduce evidence or support with *there + be* (4.8).

   (6) There **is** evidence that defense pathways for multiple stresses will simultaneously activate.

5. to show agreement with the general results of a previous paper (Hawes & Thomas, 1997).[2]

   (7) A 1999 meta-analysis of papers concerning the Mozart Effect **shows** for good that the effect **is** not due to what the researchers originally speculated (Chabris et al., 1999).

---

[2] Although it is possible for writers to use the past tense to distance themselves from a study's findings, this appears to be rare, at least in scientific writing, according to Hawes and Thomas (1997). However, notice that in Sentence 7, a past simple tense *(speculated)* is used when referring to a disproved hypothesis.

B. The past simple tense is used for two main functions in most academic fields:

   1. to introduce a specific study, usually completed by a named researcher (Swales & Feak, 2012, p. 344). The research often provides an example that supports a general statement about the topic (Hawes & Thomas, 1997).

   (8) Probably the most commonly discussed phenomenon in music cognition **is** the Mozart Effect. *[← General claim | Specific example →]* Rauscher and colleagues first **documented** the effect in their 1993 *Nature* paper.

   2. to describe the methods and data of a completed experiment. In many fields, the passive voice is commonly used in methods sections, although the active voice (with the pronoun *we*) may be possible (Sentence 10).

   (9) Statistical analyses **were used** to determine relationships between variables.

   (10) We **conducted** a secondary data analysis.

C. The past simple is usually required after any past **time marker,** such as:

     in 1997   after the war   at that time   previously

D. Although most English verbs have regular past simple forms, many of the verbs that are most common in the past simple are irregular; see Table A.2 in the Appendix.

Exercise 1: Paragraph Completion

Read this excerpt from an academic article on changes in the travel industry (Mamaghani, 2009). Choose between the present and past simple tenses, and write the correct form of the verbs in parentheses. If necessary, make sure the verb agrees with the subject.

During the pre-computerized time, the role of the travel agent

❶ _____ (be) to advise clients on travel destinations and to act as an

intermediary in the complicated process of arranging travel bookings. Even as

late as the early 1990s, consumers ❷ _____ (book) cruise travel and

tourism through travel agents as many companies ❸ _____ (no offer)

direct bookings. There ❹ _____ (be) two waves of information

technology that have had a major impact on the industry. The first of these

❺ _____ (be) the development of the direct reservation systems, such

as the American Airlines SABRE system. The second ❻ _____ (be) the

development of online sales.

By 2000, consumers no longer ❼ _____ (need) travel agents to

access the reservation system. In addition, they ❽ _____ (be) able to

manage their own travel plans efficiently. With a new structure, travel agents

❾ _____ (have) a smaller pool of individual customers that did not

wish to spend the time searching for lower-priced travel. The travel industry

❿ _____ (face) increasing threats with the dynamic pricing of online and

direct sales channels. Online travel agents, like Expedia, Lastminute, and

Ebookers, ⓫ _____ (compete) with traditional high street travel agents.

They ⓬ _____ (promise) lower costs, greater flexibility, and wider

choice. Today's travel retailers ⓭ _____ (need) increased knowledge

about product and service offerings. Knowledge ⓮ _____ (play) a key

role in not only selling breaks in recent years but cementing a customer

relationship that will mean more business in years to come.

Exercise 2: Sentence Writing

Think of an idea or finding in your field of study or research. Complete each sentence using the correct verb tense.

1. Most researchers today believe _____

   _____ .

2. It is not known whether _____

   _____ .

3. _____ years ago, most people _____ ,

   but now, _____ .

4. Generally, it is true that _____ .

   For example, _____ found that _____ .

5. In this study, the authors _____

   _____ .

Exercise 3: Vocabulary and Writing

Choose a topic from the list, and write a paragraph using as many different verbs as possible. Some suggestions are provided in parentheses; they are statistically among the most common verbs used in past and present simple tenses (see Tables A.1 and A.2 in the Appendix for a complete list of common verbs).

1. What is the role of the Internet in your field of work, research, or study? *(bring, provide, make, appear, offer, exist, reveal, consist, add, need, know, contain, allow, apply, affect)*

2. How did your field of work, research, or study first develop? *(begin, become, ask, want, occur, reveal, think, continue, need, lead, seek, start, argue, create, develop, choose, mean, fail, try, grow, allow, learn, increase, use, show, feel, tell, produce, happen)*

3. How do other people use the results or outcomes of your study, work, or research? *(use, take, become, work, depend, receive, move, include, follow, begin, try, add, tell, explain, apply, concern, enable, allow, cause, relate, run take, need)*

4. Describe an important experiment, study, book, or piece of research in your field. What did the researchers do? Why is it important? *(use, make, suggest, develop, determine, reveal, examine, demonstrate, report, conclude, address, recognize, find, result, allow, understand, indicate, mean, lead, serve, help, explain, provide, apply, illustrate, concern, relate)*

5. Choose a table or graph that interests you from a journal, magazine, or newspaper and describe it. *(show, refer, explain, mean, see, represent, tend, contain, help, note, demonstrate, change, focus, concern, relate, describe, reflect, imply, illustrate, tell, address)*

4.3: Present Perfect Tense

A. The present perfect is primarily used for referring to previous research in the field or to the writer's own previous findings. Since the present perfect is a present tense, it implies that the result is still true and relevant today. Although it is rarely required (that is, a different choice of tense would also produce a grammatical sentence), correct use of the present perfect is a sign of sophisticated and effective writing. Academic writers use the present perfect in several ways:

1. to introduce a new topic, or an entire paper or report, sometimes using *there has/have been* (4.8).

    (11) There **has been** a large body of research regarding . . . .

    (12) The percentage of part-time faculty in higher education **has grown** considerably over the last forty years.

2. to summarize previous research with general subjects, such as *researchers have found,* or *studies have suggested* (Hawes & Thomas, 1997).

    (13) Some studies **have shown** that girls have significantly higher fears than boys after trauma (Pfefferbaum et al., 1999; Pine & Cohen, 2002; Shaw, 2003). Other studies **have found** no gender differences (Rahav & Ronen, 1994).

    The present simple could also be used here, but the present perfect focuses more on *what has been done* than on *what is known to be true now* (present simple).

3. to indicate a connection between the past (what *has been* found) and the present (how you will contribute to the field).

    (14) While these measures **have proved** to be reliable and valid predictors of what they are measuring [←*previous research*], [→ *current study*] there **is** little data on how they relate to each other.

    > This is also useful when you want to point out a "gap" in the existing research. For more information, see Unit 8 of *Academic Writing for Graduate Students*, 3rd edition.

4. to describe previous findings without referring directly to the original paper, especially in the passive voice (Swales & Feak, 2012, p. 344).

    (15) **It has been shown that** biodiversity is not evenly distributed throughout the world.

    (16) Small differences in relation to trust and gender **have been** found; however, manifestations of trust across cultural contexts may differ.

    In Sentence 15, the use of *it* + passive verb + noun clause moves the result (*biodiversity is not evenly distributed*) to the "new" information position at the end of the clause (Unit 8). Similarly, in Sentence 16, the focus is on the *however* clause after the semi-colon.

5. to tell the history of an idea (what *has created* it?), describe the results of research, or draw conclusions.

(17) The framework we **have developed** will be integrated with the use of an assessment tool.

(18) This finding **has led** researchers to conclude that all the extrasolar worlds are giant gaseous planets similar to Jupiter and Saturn.

B. A small but frequently used number of verbs have irregular past participle forms (the past participle is the form of the verb after *have*); see Table A.3 in the Appendix.

Exercise 4: Vocabulary

Table A.3 in the Appendix shows the verbs that are most commonly found in perfect tenses in academic writing. Look through the list, checking the meaning of any verbs that are new to you. Then, categorize them according to some of the different functions of the present perfect tense. Write at least five verbs for each meaning:

1. To show change over time: _____

2. To introduce another writer's ideas and describe previous research: _____

   _____

3. To tell the history of an idea: _____

Exercise 5: Vocabulary and Writing

Write answers to at least three of these questions about your current reading or research using verbs from Table A.3 in the Appendix and others in the present perfect tense.

1. What have experts said about the topic? _____

   _____

2. Have there been any changes in the way your topic is understood? _____

   _____

3. What has created the current situation in your topic? _____

   _____

4. What developments have been made in your topic? _____

   _____

5. What has been concluded about your topic? _____

   _____

Exercise 6: Sentence Completion

Choose the best form of the verb in parentheses to complete the sentences.

1. In the past 20 years, the prevalence of autism (increased / has increased) dramatically.

2. This prevalence is controversial, however, since some experts question whether the diagnostic criteria for autism (expanded / have expanded).

3. Fervor (has developed / has been developed) that this increase in prevalence may be associated with childhood vaccinations.

4. The following paper (reviews / has reviewed) current research to determine if any causal relationship (has found / has been found) between autism and vaccines.

5. Vaccines as a cause of autism (were suggested / have been suggested) as early as 1995.

6. The apparent increase in autism diagnoses (coincided / has coincided) with the increase in the number of vaccines children (received / have received).

7. At that time, the American Academy of Pediatrics (recommended / has recommend) removal of thimerosal from vaccines.

8. Despite thimerosal's progressive removal from vaccines, autism rates (did not decrease / have not decreased).

4.4 Writing about the Future

A. Most academic writing focuses on discussions about previous and current research and thinking. Predictions and projections about the future occur only in particular contexts, such as calls for further research, proposals, previews in the introductions to papers, and implications sections. Most linguists argue that English has no future tense because a verb cannot be marked for the future in the same way as for past or present. As a result, there are various ways to write about the future.

B. The present simple often expresses a logical future, especially in the common phrase *further research is needed* or when previewing a paper or writing an abstract. However, there are variations, with some writers choosing *will* instead.

(19) The paper then **calls** for future research to be performed.
(20) This paper **will discuss** the power of the black-white binary as a paradigm.

C. Strong predictions about the future are expressed with the modal verb *will*. Although *will* appears regularly in academic writing, many writers prefer more cautious modal verbs such as *should* or *may* (6.1). In MICUSP, many instances of *will* report experts' strong opinions and not the graduate student writer's (Sentence 22).

> (21) In the long run, consumers **will suffer** from this lack of competition.
>
> (22) They [some of Marx's texts] all employ the same general method to show how freedom **will not come** by following the dictates of classical political economy. [It is Marx's assertion that freedom will not come in this way, not the writer's.]

D. *Will* also describes the next step in a sequence or an outcome that is predictable or proven.

> (23) Male finches **will learn** the calls of their typical host, the red-billed firefinch.[3]

E. *Be going to* is infrequent in academic writing, except in *if* clauses, where *will* is considered ungrammatical (6.4).

> (24) If a message **is going to be** a long, complicated utterance, the person doing the messaging **will break** the utterance into parts.

F. The **future-in-the-past** expresses a future action or state that happened after another time in the past. The future-in-the-past is formed with *was/were going to* or *would*.

> (25) It **became** clear the National Party **would be put out** of the majority in the South African Parliament.

Exercise 7: Writing

Choose at least two questions from the list that best fit your current studies or research. Write several sentences in response using future forms.

1. What do experts in your field predict will change or develop in the future?

2. What is a common process in your area of work? Describe it.

3. Imagine you are writing a job or university application that asks this question: What are your plans after you finish your graduate degree or current project?

4. When you were an undergraduate (or high school) student, what did you imagine you would do after graduation? Did your plans change? How?

---

[3] Finches and red-billed firefinches are birds.

4.5 Other Tenses and Verb Forms

A. The three major tenses discussed so far will be sufficient for almost all the verbs you will read and write in academic English. However, all grammar choices create different meanings, so this section considers some of the less infrequent verb forms in academic writing. Table 4.1 (page 66) contains a reminder of the formation of these tenses.

B. The present progressive describes what is happening *now* (the present simple is often timeless in its meaning). The risk with using the present progressive is that the state might not be true when your paper is actually read. The present progressive is used in writing for two main reasons:

1. to stress that an activity is ongoing at the time of writing (using verbs such as *work, try, begin, seek, develop, find, conduct, occur, ask*).

    (26) While there is not currently a vaccine for malaria, there are several that **are being developed**.

2. to show a change that is in progress at the time of the writing (using verbs such as *become, grow, increase, change, experience*).

    (27) Outside of France, the world **is changing**. Globalization **is becoming** an increasingly powerful force whose strength spares few countries.

C. The past progressive has several functions in academic writing:

1. to describe a change occurring at a time in the past, for example when describing developments in the literature.

    (28) The shifting political field that Moynihan revealed also severely constricted a wider debate on crime, which **was becoming** a large problem during the 1960s.

2. to describe actions in progress in the past, usually as part of a narrative.

    (29) Sula **was** simply **trying** out in her life what she had witnessed through direct modeling. There was nothing wrong with what she **was doing** in her mind—she **was** simply **imitating** what everyone else around her **was doing**.

3. to describe a state of events in the past, stressing that they were ongoing.

    (30) At the end of 2006, more than 39.5 million people **were living** with HIV globally.

4. to describe survey responses.

> (31) In terms of vocational status, 69 percent **were working** full time;
> 16 percent **were working** part time; 13 percent were full-time homemakers;
> 1 percent were full-time students; and 1 percent **were looking** for work.

D. The past perfect indicates an action or state that occurred before another time in the past. Therefore, it can only be used in conjunction with one or more past simple verbs. It is rare in academic writing.

> (32) REM's musical style **was** now decidedly less dissimilar with that of
> popular music; essentially alternative music **had become** the mainstream
> genre.

Many proficient writers choose the past simple in contexts where a past perfect is logically appropriate, providing the sequence of events is clear. In Sentence 33, the writer could have chosen *had ended* in the second clause, but it is clear that the game ended before the writer's arrival in the town square.

> (33) By the time we **arrived** at the town square, just 15 minutes after the
> game **ended**, there **were** already hundreds of supporters of the team there.

E. The present perfect progressive is highly infrequent in academic writing. It can be used to emphasize activities that started in the past and continue through the present (with verbs such as *try, work, study*) or changes that have not finished (e.g., *increase, grow, change*).

> (34) Kegl and other linguists **have been studying** the newly formed
> Nicaraguan Sign Language.
> (35) Online sales **have been increasing,** and current workers will soon
> fall behind in their work.

F. The past perfect progressive is even less common. It emphasizes a state or activity that was ongoing up to a point in the past. Note that progressive verbs must be capable of repetition or extension over time, so in Sentence 36 *had been diagnosed* is in the simple past perfect because it only happens once to each patient, but *had been living* extends over a period of years, and so it is in the past perfect progressive.

> (36) To test their hypothesis, experimenters examined three disease
> duration groups: patients who were diagnosed with rheumatoid arthritis
> [RA] in the past 6 months, patients who **had been living** with RA for
> a range of 1 to 7 years, and patients who **had been diagnosed** with RA
> at least 7 years ago.

G. The **past habitual** is less frequent in academic writing than in other forms of English. It is formed with *used to* or *would* plus a main verb and indicates a situation that was common in the past but is no longer true. Note that *would* can only be used with action verbs and not generally with reporting and linking verbs (Sentence 38).

(37) Florida panthers **used to have** a range that included all of the Southeastern United States.

(38) Throughout the winter and early spring of 1861, the Union revolutionaries who **would** soon **fight** the battle for Missouri were preparing for the war in hidden corners of the city.

Exercise 8: Grammatical Judgment

Choose all the possible answers to complete each sentence. Discuss how the choices change the meaning of the sentence.

_____ 1. The archeological team _____ there for almost ten years, documenting well over 1,000 sites and excavating sites of all periods. However, the researchers knew there were sites they would not have a chance to excavate, and so they allowed us to work within their concession.

   a. had worked   b. had been working   c. would work   d. worked

_____ 2. Dads _____ home from work and read the paper in silence. But a generation or two ago, they began changing diapers and reading nursery rhymes.

   a. came   b. used to come   c. had come   d. would come

_____ 3. During this interview, we asked each patient how many falls they _____ during the 6 months following their last clinic visit.

   a. experienced   b. have experience   c. had experienced   d. had been experiencing

_____ 4. Violence in the United States _____ among children and adolescents at alarming rates and is now considered a significant public health concern.

   a. is increasing   b. increased   c. has increased   d. has been increasing

_____ 5. KTNN AM 660, the Navajo Nation's official radio station, _____ plans to offer instruction in the Navajo language over the air in an attempt to follow Joshua Fishman's advice that revitalized languages, to be successful, must be shared by a people via the communications media of their communities.

   a. is making   b. made   c. has made   d. has been making

Exercise 9: Sentence Completion

Complete these sentences using your own ideas and the verb forms described in this section (past and present progressive, past perfect, past perfect progressive, present perfect progressive, habitual past). Then choose one sentence and develop it into a paragraph, using a range of appropriate verb tenses.

1. Before _____ became popular, _____.

2. In the nineteenth century, _____.

3. Until the invention of _____, people _____.

4. There has been renewed interest in _____ recently. In fact,

   _____.

4.6 Passive Voice

A. All English verb tenses have both **active** and **passive** forms. Approximately 25 percent of verbs in academic writing are in the passive voice (Biber et al., 1999). Writers use the passive voice when the subject of the clause is not the agent (Unit 1).

> *subject/goal*
> (39) These changes **were made** so the lesson would be appropriate for
> fifth grade students.

The passive is also used in clauses where the subject is not directly stated. Notice the use of the *–ing* form after a preposition (2.4).

> (40) The new plants have the same chance of **being infected**.
>
> (41) The paper focuses on people returning to the cities after **having been**
> **sent** to rural areas.

B. If the agent of the verb is important, writers often choose the active voice. However, the passive may still be a better choice if it would improve the information flow (Unit 8). In Sentence 42, the agent (*the four workers*) is moved to the new information position at the end of the sentence and then explained in the rest of the sentence.

> *subject / goal*   *agent*
> (42) The assembly line process **is conducted by four workers**, two on
> either side of the workbench, who are responsible for their own specific
> pieces of each kit.

C. The passive is formed with the finite verb *be* in the correct tense plus a past participle (see Table 4.1). Be especially careful with irregular verbs (Sentence 43) and complex verb forms such as the present perfect passive (Sentence 44):

(43a) INCORRECT: The book **was wrote** in 2009.

(43b) CORRECT: The book **was written** in 2009.

(44a) INCORRECT: New regulations **have implemented.**

(44b) CORRECT: New regulations **have been implemented.**

D. Intransitive verbs and many linking verbs do not have a passive form (1.5, 1.7).

(45a) INCORRECT: Unexpected consequences **were occurred**.

(45b) CORRECT: Unexpected consequences **occurred**.

E. There are two useful passive structures with reporting verbs (3.3); a common error is to confuse them (Sentence 46c).

> The passive is also very important in descriptions of processes. See Unit 3 (pages 119–125) of *Academic Writing for Graduate Students*, 3rd edition.

(46a) **It** is thought **that** the plague killed 25 percent of Europeans in the 14th century.

(46b) **The plague** is thought **to have killed** 25 percent of Europeans in the 14th century.

(46c) INCORRECT: **The plague** is thought **that** 25 percent of Europeans were killed.

F. Overuse of the passive: Using too many passive voice verbs can make writing sound impersonal because there will be few agents. Varying sentences with some verbs in the active voice may be preferable. However, there are some verbs that are rarely used in the passive voice even though they are transitive (see Table 4.2).

Table 4.2 Common Verbs That Are Never (in bold) or Rarely Used in the Passive Voice					
appear	consist	happen	last	resemble	stay
arrive	come	fall	occur	rest	wait
belong	die	lack	remain	seem	

Based on Hinkel, 2004, p. 163.

G. Avoiding personal pronouns: Although many students have been advised not to use *I* or *we* in their writing, some journals now encourage the use of personal pronouns, partly to prevent excessive use of the passive voice.

> (47) **We** hope that **our** model will inform the fields of biodiversity monitoring, biological research, and science education.

We refers to the multiple authors of the paper, not *you* and *me* (the reader and writer).

Exercise 10: Paragraph Revision

Read this paragraph adapted from a literature review on the history of smartphones. Then complete the tasks.

The first super-powered phone ❶ <u>was called</u> Simon, which was "8 inches long, weigh[ed] 1 pound, [had] 1 megabyte of memory, and [. . .] cost $1,000" (Maney, 1993). ❷ <u>It was thought to be</u> a computer with "communication capability" (Maney, 1993), rather than a phone. However, even the feature phones today are smaller and more powerful. ❸ <u>IBM unveiled it</u> as a PDA (Personal Digital Assistant) in 1992, because there was no smartphone concept until 1997, when ❹ <u>Ericsson released the first smart phone</u> ("History," 2010). In 2002, focused on business executives, ❺ <u>Research In Motion (RIM) introduced the first BlackBerry</u>, which was the first phone capable of sending and receiving email, which is the core service of RIM today. In the same year, ❻ <u>Sony Ericsson released the first camera smart phone</u> trying to attract entertainment consumers. Since this device, ❼ <u>new hardware has been installed</u> on smartphones, like GPS, Wi-Fi, gyroscopes, and accelerometers.

1. Which of the verbs in the underlined clauses could the writer change from active to passive or passive to active in order to improve the old-to-new information flow of the paragraph (see 8.1)? (Some clauses do not need to be changed.)

   _____

   _____

   _____

2. Rewrite the improved paragraph on a separate piece of paper.

Exercise 11: Editing

Correct the errors in the use and form of the passive voice.

1. Cell phones have been thought that they would replace laptops for some functions.

2. Consumers have been attracting to smartphones by their low prices.

3. However, a two-year agreement requires for actual phone service.

4. Because people are using features like web browsing so much, unlimited data plans, which used to make available as standard, are now disappearing.

5. After the phone hacking scandal in the U.K. was happened, phone makers began reminding customers to set a secure password on their phones.

6. Some phones can use as a GPS navigation device.

Exercise 12: Vocabulary and Writing

Tables A.4 and A.5 in the Appendix show the most frequent verbs found in the passive voice in academic writing. Use them to write answers on a separate piece of paper to these prompts, using passive voice where appropriate.

1. Describe a common process in your field of study, work, or research. For example, you could describe an experimental technique, a statistical test, or a workplace activity. How is it done? How is it used?

2. Describe an important modern invention. When, where, why, and how was it made? How is it used? What is it expected to achieve? What is it related to? How is it regarded?

3. Imagine you are giving an award to a famous scholar, practitioner, or celebrity. Why was this person chosen for the award? What criteria is the decision based on? How is the person described by other people? Why is the person being presented with an award? Who has the person been compared to?

4.7 Common Problems with Verb Tenses

A. Choosing a default tense: In academic writing, the present simple is usually preferred unless you have a good reason to use a different tense. If your clause is essentially timeless (the verb is general or factual), choose the present simple.

B. Changing tenses: It is common to use different tenses in the same paragraph or even sentence, but there must always be a clear reason for the shift, such as an adverb or prepositional phrase of time (*since, in 2007*, etc.).

C. Overuse of *be:* Writers from certain language backgrounds tend to insert *be* where it is not needed, for example, in present and past simple tenses. *Be* is only correctly used: (1) as a main verb; (2) in the progressive aspect; and (3) in the passive voice.

D. Present perfect with past time markers: Since the present perfect is a present tense, it is incorrect after past time markers such as *in 2001, ten years ago, in the past, before that,* and *at that time.* These markers require a past simple or (less frequently) a past perfect tense.

E. Required present perfect: The present (or past) perfect must be used after time markers using the prepositions *since* and *for. Since* introduces a specific time (*since 2001*); *for* indicates a period of time (*for centuries*).

Exercise 13: Paragraph Writing

Answer the questions in a paragraph or two on a separate piece of paper, paying particular attention to the verb tenses.

1. What *is* your current research topic?

2. What *have* experts already *learned* about this topic?

3. Choose one research article. What *did* it *find*?

4.8 Subject-Verb Agreement

A. English verbs **agree** in number (singular or plural) in the present simple, present perfect, and all progressive and passive forms. Subject-verb agreement may require some attention in certain cases.

B. When the subject and verb are separated, the verb always agrees with the head noun (1.2). This may not be the closest noun to the verb. Generally, look to the left to find the head noun.

> (48) After WWII, the rapid **advancement** of military and space technolo-
> gies **was** deemed crucial to countering the Soviet threat.

C. Indefinite pronouns are always singular (*some/any/no/every* + *one/body/thing/time*). Some other pronouns are always singular (*none,*[4] *each, every, one, little*), while others are always plu-ral (*all, both, some, few, most, many*).

> (49) Under common coordination, **each is** doing his own assignments and
> simultaneously shares information with others.

D. When the subject is a clause, the verb is singular.

> (50) What this means in practice **is** that MTCT must be combated at
> multiple stages of pregnancy and birth.

E. The verb in a relative clause agrees with the referent if the subject is a relative pronoun (Sentence 51). Non-restrictive relative clauses that refer to an entire clause or idea are always singular (Sentence 52).

> (51) The unemployment rate does not include **people who are** no
> longer looking for jobs.
> (52) The characters are two professors, which **suggests** that their
> interaction is somewhat formal.

---

[4] *None* is often used with a plural verb in spoken English, informal writing, and even in some formal contexts.

F. A compound subject joined with *and* is plural because the subject contains at least two items (X + Y). In the case of *or* (including *either . . . or, neither . . . nor*), the verb agrees with the *last* noun.

> (53) A "grip of print" occurs when course curriculum or **ideas are** fixed into text.

> (54) . . . if nutrients or **water becomes** limiting.

G. When using the clause structure *there + be,* the verb agrees with the complement.

> (55) There **is** no **effect** on the trade balance overall.

> (56) There **are** three main **ways** cities commonly maintain strong economic sustainability.

This structure can be used in any tense and also with modal verbs and in non-finite clauses. It is generally used to introduce a new idea, summarize previous research, or start a list.

> (57) We predict that **there will be** a large amount of variation in ecosystem response.

> (58) **There have been** no empirical studies thus far testing the utility of Bronfenbrenner's ecology model of human development.

> (59) Therefore, calculations were continued, **there being** no need for additional reconsideration.

There can also be used with the verbs *exist, remain, arise, occur, follow,* and *ensue* (Halliday, 1994, p. 142).

Exercise 14: Editing

Choose the correct form of the verbs in parentheses to complete these sentences from an article on psycholinguistic research at the University of Michigan ("Mild, um, speech pauses are persuasive," 2011).

1. A new study (find / finds) that people who spoke, fast, but not too fast; with a pitch, but not too high or low; and with a few short pauses (was / were) the most successful in convincing the listener to take a desired action.

2. Interviewers who spoke moderately fast, at a rate of about 3.5 words per second, (was / were) much more successful at getting people to agree.

3. People who (talk / talks) really fast (is / are) seen as fast-talkers out to pull the wool over our eyes, and people who (talk / talks) really slow (is / are) seen as not too bright or overly pedantic.

4. Too much pitch variation (sounds / sound) artificial.

5. Pitch, the highness or lowness of voices, (is / are) a highly gendered quality of speech.

6. The last speech characteristic the researchers examined for the study (was / were) the use of pauses.

7. Here they found that interviewers who engaged in frequent short pauses (was / were) more successful than those who (was / were) perfectly fluent.

8. The researchers plan to compare the speech of the most and least successful interviewers to see how the content of conversations, as well as measures of speech quality, (is / are) related to their success rates.

Exercise 15: Sentence Completion

Complete the sentences with your own ideas using a present tense. Choose the correct subject-verb agreement from the choices in parentheses.

1. There (has/have) been few studies _____.

2. What is surprising (is/are) that _____.

3. Neither the authors nor the reviewer _____.

4. None of _____.

5. Experts who have studied this question _____.

6. There are several reasons _____.

7. Further research (is/are) needed, which _____.

8. In the future, there may _____.

9. There (is/are) evidence that _____.

10. There (is/are) two ways _____.

4.9 Subject-Verb Inversion

A. A small number of adverbs cause the subject and verb to switch places (that is, invert) when they are moved to the start of a clause. Most of the adverbs have a negative meaning. Since this structure moves a word into an unusual position at the start of the clause, inverted sentences sound more emphatic, and the adverb is given more weight.

> (60) **Not only do Filipino teachers** have to deal with larger class sizes, they also have to teach many more hours.
>
> (61) While politicians and organizations fighting for change might go to great lengths to relay its benefits, **rarely do they target** their campaign at the ideology behind resistance.
>
> (62) **Only then can the work** toward a fusion of horizons commence.

Notice that main verbs that do not have a separate auxiliary verb in regular (subject-verb) word order require *do/does/did* when they invert (Sentences 60 and 61).

B. A frequent and useful structure is *not only . . . but also*. It is used to add a new—and often surprising—piece of information to an existing idea. As with all these structures, *not only . . . but also* is used with regular word order when the adverb is not at the start of the clause (Sentences 63 and 64).

> (63) We must consider **not only** the native species, **but also** the dynamic ecosystems.
>
> (64) Immunoglobulins **not only** attach to the surfaces of fungi marking them for extermination, **but also** neutralize dangerous mycotoxins released by the fungi.

C. A slightly different form of inversion is possible with some linking verbs (1.7). In this case, the subject and complement are reversed. In some cases, this would create a passive clause, but the verb *be* has no passive form, so the effect is similar to an inversion.

For more information on using inversion for emphasis, see Unit 6 (page 269) of *Academic Writing for Graduate Students*, 3rd edition.

> (65) **Particularly important are** plans that not only achieve financial objectives but meet customer satisfaction and performance criteria as well.

Exercise 16: Sentence Rewriting

Rewrite these sentences using the words provided. Some, but not all, require inversion.

1. Tracking not only hurts the members of the lowest track, it also hurts members of the upper track.

   Not only _____

2. Women rarely owned land without a husband to share ownership.

   Rarely _____

3. Their management style was sometimes misinterpreted.

   Sometimes _____

4. True economic growth will only occur then.

   Only then _____

5. We should not only consider the cost, but also other relevant issues.

   Not only _____

6. The capability to keep stored data is especially useful.

   Especially useful _____

Grammar in Your Discipline

A. Look through a literature review in your field of study (from the introduction to a journal article, an early chapter of a dissertation, or an entire published review article) and find examples of:

   1. references to sources using present simple, present perfect, and past simple tenses

   2. a sentence with a different tense in the main (reporting) clause and (subordinate) noun clause

   3. verb tenses other than the present simple, present perfect, and past simple

B. Look again at your literature review and answer these questions.

   1. Which tenses are most common in your texts? Why? _____

   _____

   2. If tenses other than the three most common ones are used, can you explain why?

   _____

   _____

3. Do writers in your field use personal pronouns (*I, we, you*)? If so, can see you any patterns?

_____

_____

C. Share your findings with a small group of writers from other disciplines. Do you notice any similarities or differences?

D. Write a review of the literature on a topic of interest, importance, or controversy in your field. You may need to conduct secondary research to find more sources. Ask your instructor for directions as to the length and detail of your review as well as the type and number of sources required. Edit your writing carefully for common errors in verb tense, passive voice, and subject-verb agreement.

> For more information about literature reviews, including forms of citations, see Units 5 and 8 of *Academic Writing for Graduate Students*, 3rd edition, as well as *Telling a Research Story* (Feak & Swales, 2009).

The Noun Phrase

Noun phrases appear as subjects, complements, and objects of prepositions. Noun phrases in academic writing are often long and complex: while the verb controls the structure of the clause, the noun phrases carry its content, so they contain a lot of information. One of the most difficult aspects of the noun phrase for non-native speakers of English is the article system, which is discussed in this unit.

UNIT 5 Preview Test

Write *a, an, the, this, these, its,* or Ø (no article) on each line. More than one choice may be grammatical. Discuss your choices.

Florida Panther Conservation

1 _____ Florida panthers have been put under **2** _____ extreme stress as **3** _____ result of **4** _____ human impacts. **5** _____ habitat fragmentation, **6** __/__ busy highways, and **7** __/__ limits on immigration are just **8** _____ few of **9** _____ problems faced by **10** _____ panther. **11** _____ panther populations have been in **12** _____ decline, but there is **13** _____ hope for **14** _____ populations. In order to better assist **15** _____ Florida panther, scientists must look at and understand **16** _____ life history traits, including **17** _____ survival rates, **18** _____ age of maturation, and **19** _____ age structure of **20** _____ population. We looked in-depth at each of **21** _____ factors, and used them to find out how each factor affects **22** _____ growth and decline of **23** _____ panther populations.

Grammar Awareness: Title and Abstract

Read the title and abstract from a student's economics research paper (included in MICUSP). Then complete the tasks.

**Pooled Signals:
The Effect of Competitive Admissions
Processes on College Choice**

Abstract

❶ This paper looks at the problem of college choice in an environment with heterogeneous agents, competitive admissions processes, and post-graduation wages dependent on college reputation. ❷ It is demonstrated that under certain regularity conditions, a separating equilibrium where all the top agents attend the college with the good reputation while weaker agents attend the lesser college exists and is unique. ❸ This result is incorporated in a simple dynamic model, which shows that initially identical institutions may become differentiated over time, and that this may be hard to reverse. ❹ Finally, the model is applied to race-based admissions policies and used to analyze the distributional effects of such policies.

1. Circle all the finite verbs in the abstract and highlight their subjects.

2. Look again at the title. What is its grammatical structure? Is it a complete sentence? In your experience, is this typical of papers in your discipline?

3. Explain the use of the underlined determiners in these excerpts from the abstract (∅ = no article):

   a. The problem of college choice _____

   b. an environment with heterogeneous choices _____

   c. while ∅ weaker agents . . . _____

   d. This result is incorporated in . . . _____

   e. a simple dynamic model _____

   f. ∅ over time _____

   g. Finally, the model is applied to . . . _____

   h. ∅ race-based admissions policies _____

5.1 Count and Non-Count Nouns

A. Nouns can be divided into two main categories of meaning: **common** nouns and **proper** nouns. Proper nouns include the names of people, places, books, journals, businesses, and organizations, and they start with a capital letter (Isaac Newton, Australia, *Nature*, Google). All other nouns are common nouns. Common nouns can be divided into two further categories: **count** and **non-count** nouns (Figure 5.1). There is a difference in meaning between count and non-count nouns: count nouns can be separated into individual units and counted (e.g., *book, computer, student*); non-count nouns exist as masses and abstract quantities that cannot be counted (e.g., *research, water, information*).

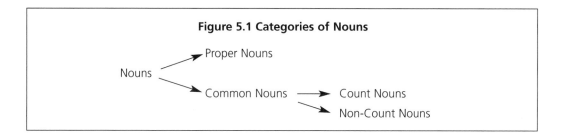

Figure 5.1 Categories of Nouns

B. Most English nouns are regular, count nouns. Non-count nouns and nouns with **irregular** plurals are exceptions. However, non-count nouns occur frequently in academic texts. Although it is possible to categorize non-count nouns by their meaning (e.g., chemical elements, abstract nouns, and category words), it may be easier to use Hinkel's (2004) system of identifying non-count nouns by their suffix (ending), as shown in Table 5.1 on page 92. This is not a complete list—there are many non-count nouns that do not fit these patterns, but all the examples given are high-frequency nouns in academic writing.

C. The distinction between count and non-count nouns is important because of three grammatical features:

1. Only count nouns can be made plural.
2. Count and non-count nouns permit different quantifiers (5.6).
3. Singular count nouns must have a word in the *determiner* slot, for example, *a, the, this,* or a possessive noun (1.2).

Table 5.1 Major Categories of Non-Count Nouns		
Non-Count Forms	**Examples (Non-Count/Uncountable)**	**Exceptions (Count)**
-work	homework, coursework, work, fieldwork	*a framework, a network, a work of art*
-age	courage, postage, luggage, baggage, barrage, garbage	*a garage*
-edge	knowledge	
-ice	advice, juice, practice, ice	
-ware	hardware, software, silverware	
-fare	welfare, warfare	
-th	health, wealth, strength, truth, youth	*a myth*
-(ol)ogy, -try	biology, psychology, chemistry, geometry	
Abstract nouns: *-ance/-ence* *-ness* *-(s/t)ure* *-(i)ty / -cy* *and also . . .*	chance *(luck),* tolerance, competence happiness, hopelessness closure, moisture, tenure cruelty, honesty, gravity information, atmosphere, alcohol, equipment, pollution, logic	*a chance* *a measure*
-ing	reading, smoking, drinking	
Nouns that are the same as verbs	smoke, help, water, traffic, weather, work, labor, consent, research, trade, traffic	
Nouns that only exist as nouns	art, business, energy, fun, grammar, music, oxygen, trouble, vocabulary, wisdom, prestige	

(Adapted from Hinkel, 2004, p. 106)

D. Some non-count nouns also exist in a countable form. These can be called **double nouns** because they change from non-count to count with a slightly different meaning. The non-count form refers to the whole idea or quantity, whereas the count noun refers to a specific example or type. Once the double noun is countable, it can be used with the indefinite articles *a* or *an* or made plural.

Non-Count	*Count*
(1a) Linguistics is the study of **language**.	(1b) English is **an** international **language**.
(2a) The course requires a lot of **work**.	(2b) The book is **a work** of literature.
(3a) Children need **structure**.	(3b) These are traditional family **structures**.

E. With many other non-count nouns, you can use a count noun of quantity as the head noun, moving the non-count noun into a prepositional phrase (e.g., *a piece of research, a glass of water*).

F. A very small number of countable nouns have irregular plurals. Some of the most frequent are *man/men, woman/women, child/children, foot/feet, tooth/teeth, criterion/criteria, phenomenon/phenomena, datum/data.*[1]

Exercise 1: Grammatical Awareness

Determine if the nouns are count (C) or non-count (NC) in their most common usage.

1. C / NC student	11. C / NC process
2. C / NC time	12. C / NC development
3. C / NC study	13. C / NC information
4. C / NC year	14. C / NC experience
5. C / NC school	15. C / NC health
6. C / NC group	16. C / NC behavior
7. C / NC system	17. C / NC history
8. C / NC education	18. C / NC law
9. C / NC research	19. C / NC relationship
10. C / NC community	20. C / NC value

---

[1] Although *datum* as a singular is highly infrequent, many academic writers recognize *data* as a plural noun and use plural verbs (e.g., *the data suggest*).

Exercise 2: Sentence Writing

Write sentences using the following double nouns (a) as non-count nouns and (b) as count nouns. Use a dictionary if you are not sure how the meaning varies between count and non-count forms.

1. experience

    a. _____

    b. _____

2. speech

    a. _____

    b. _____

3. environment (as a non-count noun, *environment* requires the article *the*; see 5.5)

    a. _____

    b. _____

4. change

    a. _____

    b. _____

5. education

    a. _____

    b. _____

5.2 Articles

A. **Articles** (*the, a, an*) are the most common **determiners.** Their function in the noun phrase is to determine or specify whether the head noun is general or specific in its reference: is it all things, one of many things, or this one thing?[2] The choice of article largely depends on whether the writer and/or the reader know the exact reference of the noun (see Table 5.2).

B. The article *the* is about twice as common as *a/an* in academic writing (Biber et al., 1999). This is probably because writing at this level is very concerned with broad ideas and categories (generic reference, usually no article) and specific details (definite reference, always *the*).

Table 5.2 Articles and Reference (Ø = no article)			
		Reader	
		doesn't know which one(s)	knows which one(s)
Writer	doesn't know which one(s)	**Generic Reference** (5.4)[3] **(=all of it/them)** *Singular count* → *a/an, the* *Plural and non-count* → Ø the human brain a leader science	**Indefinite Reference** (5.4) **(=one/some of many)** *Singular count* → *a/an* *Plural and non-count* → Ø use a computer (=*your computer*)[4]
	knows which one(s)	**Indefinite Reference** (5.4) **(=one/some of many)** *Singular count* → *a/an* *Plural and non-count* → Ø a new technique different options there is disagreement	**Definite Reference** (5.5) **(=this/these exactly)** *all common nouns* → *the* the main office the best advice the participants

Adapted from Brown (1973) and Celce-Murcia & Larsen Freeman (1999, p. 282).

---

[2] I am grateful to Dr. Gigi Taylor for explaining the article system to me in this way. Her description of articles can be found at http://writingcenter.unc.edu/handouts/articles/.

[3] Arguably, some indefinite references fall into this category, too (e.g., *Start your paper with an abstract*); however, the distinction is not important for choosing the correct article.

[4] This quadrant is hard to find in academic writing because writers rarely write about things known only to the reader. Celce-Murcia and Larsen-Freeman's (1999) examples include *I heard you once wrote an article on X* (p. 282).

Exercise 3: Grammar Analysis

These sentences are taken from an abstract on the topic of MP3 compression quality (MP3 is a computer sound file format). Look at the phrases in bold in the chart. Decide if the reader knows the reference. Write Y for Yes or N for No in the column. Then do the same for the writer. Then identify the type of reference: generic (G), indefinite (I), or definite (D).

> This paper shows a practical application of a general factorial experiment to analyze the interactions between important controllable factors in the creation of high-quality compressed (MP3) music files. Traditional sound quality experiments depend on listeners' subjective opinions and this experiment instead utilizes an objective measure of fidelity based on digital signal analysis of an encoded and decoded music file compared with the original clip.

	Writer Knows?	Reader Knows?	Generic, Indefinite, Definite?
1. This paper shows **a practical application**			
2. of **a general factorial experiment**			
3. to analyze **the interactions**			
4. between **important controllable factors**			
5. in **the creation**			
6. of **high-quality compressed (MP3) music files.**			
7. **Traditional sound quality experiments**			
8. depend on **listeners' subjective opinions**			
9. and this experiment instead utilizes **an objective measure**			
10. of **fidelity**			
11. based on **digital signal analysis**			
12. of **an encoded and decoded music file**			
13. compared with **the original clip.**			

5.3 Generic Reference

A. Nouns that describe a class, not an individual person or thing, have **generic reference**; the meaning of the noun is *all of it/them*. Generic reference can often be seen in general statements used to introduce, define, or summarize ideas.

> (4) Until fairly recently, **discussions** of English as a Second Language (ESL) **issues** in composition **studies** have been few and far between.[5]

B. With **non-count nouns**, use *no* article for generic reference:

> (5) The development of a testable hypothesis is a key characteristic of good **science**.

C. With **count** nouns, you have three choices for generic reference.

1. Use a plural noun (with no article). This the most common choice for generic reference.

> (6) The process can be intensely demoralizing both for **students** and **teachers.**

2. Use *a/an* + singular noun, especially in definitions. Notice the structure of Sentence 7: generic noun (term) + linking verb + indefinite noun (category) + relative clause. This structure distinguishes the term from other members of the same category.

> For more practice with definitions, see Unit 2 of *Academic Writing for Graduate Students,* 3rd edition, and Appendix One.

> (7) **A portfolio** is a file containing samples of a child's work.[6]

3. Use *the* + singular noun as an alternative with humans, animals, organs of the body, plants, and complex inventions. It is used only in formal contexts. In Sentence 8 notice that the use of the singular noun *the adolescent* requires both personal pronouns (*his or her*). The plural (*adolescents*) would permit a single pronoun *(their).*

> (8) The basic structure of **the brain** is affected by the sum of **the adolescent**'s experiences with his or her environment.

---

[5] Non-native speakers of English might be interested to know that Sentences 4, 9, 10, and 11 are taken from an influential journal article published by a graduate student (now a professor) who identifies himself as a "second language writer" (Matsuda, 1999, p. 718).

[6] The category noun *(file)* is indefinite rather than generic because all portfolios (generic) are files of children's work, but not all files are portfolios.

Exercise 4: Sentence Completion

A. Complete the sentences by choosing the best form in parentheses to express generic reference.

1. I investigated whether (a gender stereotype / gender stereotypes) at a conscious and non-conscious level are causing (women / the woman) to perform worse than (a man / men) in their mathematics classes.

2. Some define (creativity / a creativity) simply as "the ability to produce (work / a work) which is both novel and appropriate" (Lubart, 1994).

3. (Divergent thinking / Divergent thinkings) encourages (the individual / the individuals) to think of as many ideas as possible.

4. (The gender identity development / Gender identity development) is one of the most crucial milestones that (a child / child) attains.

5. (The turbulence / Turbulence) may be studied by examining the fluid velocity fields in (the internal combustion engines / internal combustion engines).

B. Identify three nouns from the passage that could be rewritten using a different grammatical choice for generic structure (e.g., *individuals* can be rewritten as *an individual* or *the individual*).

1. _____

2. _____

3. _____

Exercise 5: Sentence Writing

Choose any five of the common nouns in academic English from the box and write sentences using them with generic reference.

client	culture	education	leader	research
conflict	evidence	facility	practice	skill

1. _____

2. _____

3. _____

4. _____

5. _____

5.4 Indefinite Reference

A. Indefinite reference is appropriate when the reader and/or the writer do not *both* know the specific identity of the noun. This might be because it is not important (*use a computer = use any computer*), not known to the writer (*further study is needed*), or new to the reader (*we used a new technique*—the writer knows exactly which technique, but the reader doesn't). The basic meaning of a noun with indefinite reference (**indefinite article**) is *one or some out of many.*

> (9) In **a review** of empirical research comparing ESL writers and native speakers of English . . . [The writer knows the review well, but it is a new reference for the reader.]
>
> (10) Prior to the 1940s, the teaching of ESL was not regarded as **a profession** in the United States. [*A profession* here means "any profession," so the noun is indefinite.]

B. Use *a/an* for all singular count nouns with indefinite reference. Remember to use *an* when the next word starts with a vowel sound. Non-count nouns and plural nouns with this meaning have no article.

> (11) The presence of **ESL students** should be **an important consideration** for all teachers and scholars of writing because **ESL students** can be found in **many writing courses** across the United States.

C. Note that in practice, it is difficult (and probably not necessary) to distinguish between generic and indefinite reference for non-count and plural nouns since they use the same grammatical choices. In Sentence 11, *ESL students* is indefinite because it means *some* ESL students, not all of them everywhere, but *all teachers and scholars* and *writing* are both generic because they refer to categories, not groups or particular examples.

D. Two special uses of indefinite reference are:

1. expressions of quantity (*a* number of, *a* piece of, *a* section of)
2. the meaning of *per* (60 miles an hour; $200 an hour)

Exercise 6: Sentence Completion

Complete the paragraph adapted from the methods section of a research report by adding *a* or *an*, if necessary, or Ø if no article is required.

❶ _____ participants were first asked to take ❷ _____ piece of paper from ❸ _____ bag. The paper contained ❹ _____ number which assigned them to one of the two groups. Then the participants entered the room and were asked to take ❺ _____ seat at one of the seats with ❻ _____ survey. One of the experimenters then went around the room with ❼ _____ bundle of pencils and ❽ _____ participants were asked to take one to fill out the survey. Upon completion, ❾ _____ surveys and ❿ _____ pencils were collected by ⓫ _____ experimenter. ⓬ _____ short video clip was then shown. For the subliminal group ⓭ _____ subliminal message was inserted into the video; ⓮ _____ red background was also used for the computer screen. For the nonsubliminal group no message was flashed during the video, and ⓯ _____ white background was used during the playing of the video. At the conclusion of the video clip, ⓰ _____ post-survey was passed out, to ⓱ _____ participants. ⓲ _____ bundle of pens was also handed out, and ⓳ _____ participants were asked to choose ⓴ _____ pen. There were 45 pens total, with 15 blue, black, and red pens each.

5.5 Definite Reference

A. Definite reference is used when the reader and writer both know or can easily find the exact meaning of the noun. Academic writers use definite reference extensively to connect ideas within and between sentences and to establish shared knowledge with readers. All common nouns (count and non-count, singular and plural) use *the* (as the **definite article**) for definite reference.

B. A noun is definite if:

1. it has been previously identified in the text.

(12) Payne et al. conducted their first cross foster experiment in 1998: Payne and his colleagues performed **the experiment** with *Vidua chalybeata*, the village indigobird. [*The experiment* is definite in the second sentence because it was introduced in the first.]

2. it is unique (if there is only one of something, it is fully identified for the reader).

    (13) a large negative impact on **the environment**

3. the noun phrase includes a superlative adjective, which is necessarily unique (*the first, the second, the next, the only*, etc.).

    (14) **The biggest problem** is lack or waste of money.

4. the noun is fully identified by a modifier or qualifier (*the* U.S. government; *the* problem of college choice; *the* people who supported Réunion's close association with France). Sometimes, however, a qualifier (restrictive relative clause or prepositional phrase) does not always make the noun definite, for example, in a definition such as Sentence 7.]

5. the noun is part of a whole group.

    (15) The agricultural sector accounts for about one-fourth of **the** country's Gross Domestic Product (GDP), two-fifths of **the** country's exports, and half of **the** labor force.

C. Note that a small number of proper nouns also require definite articles (*the Atlantic Ocean, the Antarctic, the White House*), including some countries or territories that are or were comprised of smaller units (*the United States, the United Kingdom, the Philippines, the Soviet Union*). Another rare exception to the general pattern of not using any articles with proper nouns is to suggest that a person or organization changed over time (Sentence 16). These nouns must be qualified with a restrictive relative clause or prepositional phrase.

    (16) Europe is not today what it was when President Bush took office, and it scarcely resembles **the Europe that** President Bill Clinton claimed to know. [The writer distinguishes between Europe today and the Europe of the past.]

Exercise 7: Sentence Completion

Use Table 5.2 on page 95 to complete the chart. Write Y for Yes if the writer knows the referent or N for No. Do the same for the reader. Decide if the noun is count (C), proper (P), or plural (Pl). Then choose the best article (or choose no article, Ø) for these phrases from the start of a news report in *Science* (Cohen, 2009). Write it on the line in Column 1.

	Writer Knows?	Reader Knows?	What Kind of Noun?
1. On 24 August, _____ government			
2. released _____ report			
3. about _____ swine flu pandemic			
4. from _____ group			
5. of _____ prominent scientists			
6. commissioned by _____ U.S. President Barack Obama.			
7. _____ first report issued by . . .			

Exercise 8: Writing

Write a paragraph explaining why you chose to study in your current field or take a piece of unedited writing you wrote recently. Underline all the head nouns in your writing and circle all the articles. For each noun, check whether it is fully identified to the reader and/or writer, and what type of noun it is (proper, non-count, singular count, plural). Use Table 5.2 to correct any errors.

5.6 Quantifiers

A. **Quantifiers** add information about the number or amount of the head noun. Some quantifiers are restricted to certain types of nouns (plural count nouns or non-count nouns) (Table 5.3).

Table 5.3 Common Quantifiers	
Non-Count Nouns	**Plural Count Nouns**
(a) little	(a) few
a great deal of	several
a large amount of	a large number of
(too) much	(too) many
Both Non-Count and Plural Count Nouns	
no / none of	
hardly any	
some	
a lot of	
(almost) all	

B. Be careful with the adverb *too*; it means "in excess." For example, if an experiment takes *too much time*, you cannot possibly complete it. Compare this with *so*, which means a lot, but not too much. Noun phrases or adjectives with *too* can be followed by a non-finite *to* clause, which describes a goal that cannot be reached.

(17) There are far **too many variables** at work **to predict** with confidence the full, long-term impact of modern tools of communications.

C. There is an important difference between *little/few* (almost none) and *a little/a few* (some, but not many/much):

(18a) places where there is **a little** discrimination *[some]*

(18b) there is **little** consensus *[almost none]*

(19a) **a few** students have benefited *[some]*

(19b) there are **few** clear guidelines *[almost none]*

In Sentence 18a, discrimination is said to exist, whereas in Sentence 18b, the reader can assume that there is almost no consensus. In Sentence 19a, some students have benefitted, so the sentence has a positive meaning, while in Sentence 19b, there is a lack of guidelines, and the sentence has a negative meaning.

D. *A lot of* is somewhat informal, occurring 20 times more frequently in spoken English than academic writing, where *much* or *many* are often chosen instead.

E. Notice the difference between *a number of people* (where **people** is the head noun) and *the number of people* (where **number** is the head noun):

(20) a number of **studies** *have* noted . . .

(21) the **number** of factors *was* limited to 10 . . .

F. A noun phrase with a quantifier can also include a definite article (*the*), **possessive determiner,** or **specific determiner** (*this, these, that, those*). Those make the noun more specific. In Sentences 22 and 23, the definite articles show that the nouns are fully identified in the text (not any measures, but specifically the measures taken to protect records, in Sentence 22) or familiar to the reader (in Sentence 23, the reader is expected to share the writer's understanding of the business community). In Sentence 24, the possessive *his* limits the nouns *data and ideas* to Darwin's.

(22) **Some of the measures** taken to protect records will be technology based.

(23) There is an antagonism between environmental protection and **much of the** business community.

(24) Darwin's discussions of species never pulled **all his data and ideas** together into an explicit theory about what species are and how new ones originate.

The preposition *of* is required for most quantifiers in this pattern; *all* is an exception because the preposition is optional, but *of* is omitted after *all* about twice as often as it is used, according to the Corpus of Contemporary American English. Be careful not to omit the definite article with other quantifiers (not *most of students*).

G. The expression *one of the* + plural noun is very frequent in academic writing. This is not a quantifier as such: *one* is actually the head noun and will agree with the verb (4.8). However, the noun must be plural because the meaning is "one out of many things."

> (25a) INCORRECT: **One of the consideration** in comparing the interventions is their cost.

> (25b) CORRECT: **One of the considerations** in comparing the interventions is their cost.

Exercise 9: Sentence Completion

Choose the best word in the parentheses to complete the sentences.

1. The youths were hesitant to share (many / much) details about the family conflict.

2. A traffic jam is caused by having (so / too) many cars on the road.

3. Cichlid fish have attracted (a great deal / much) of attention from evolutionary biologists.

4. One of the (reason / reasons) for the increase in interracial dating (is / are) that there has been a greater minority enrollment in colleges and universities.

5. Because (few / a few) people learn anything completely the first time, the practice step is really an iterative process where the trainee gets some of it right, tries again, and gets more right, and so on.

6. Many options for instruction exist for the teacher who is willing to spend (little / a little) time organizing the program.

7. Scientific and technological knowledge have grown enormously since the Greeks embarked on the scientific venture in the sixth century BCE, but during these 25 centuries there has been (plenty of / hardly any) progress in the conduct of social affairs.

8. Although the number of animals in captivity (is / are) large, their genetic variability is relatively low.

Exercise 10: Sentence Writing

Write sentences using these phrases with your own ideas and information. All the phrases are used frequently in academic writing.

1. few experts

   _____

2. a number of reasons

   _____

3. a great deal of time

   _____

4. hardly any evidence

   _____

5. several factors

   _____

6. one of the best examples

   _____

7. a large amount of information

   _____

8. all levels

   _____

9. too much attention

   _____

10. a little help

   _____

5.7 Adjectives

A. Although adjectives are usually associated with types of language that value description (such as speech or fiction), the corpus shows that adjectives are more frequent in academic writing than any other discourse. In fact, adjectives occur almost twice as frequently in academic writing as in spoken English. Academic writing also uses a greater range of adjectives than any other type of English.

B. The most common adjectives in the academic section of the Corpus of Contemporary American English are shown in Table 5.4.

Table 5.4 Top Adjectives in Academic Writing (in order of frequency)				
other	national	good	higher	likely
new	high	cultural	small	specific
social	economic	environmental	military	similar
political	human	local	early	white
American	public	physical	major	individual
important	significant	large	black	current
different	international	possible	great	common

C. Adjectives can have two different functions in the noun phrase: they can **describe** the quality of the noun (*good, new, black, white, great*), or they can **classify** the noun (*social, economic, public, cultural*). Table 5.4 suggests that the second, classifying function is especially important in academic writing.

> (26) Emerging markets are now entering this arena and will become **significant** players. [descriptive] [7]
>
> (27) There is no evidence of **social** hierarchy prior to this period. [classifying]

D. Usually, descriptive adjectives are written before classifying ones; that is, adjectives describing an opinion or attitude precede more objective ones.

> (28) Better communication could lead to **positive educational** reforms.
>
> (29) This study will add **important new** information to the field.

---

[7] In some disciplines, *significant* always means *statistically significant*, that is, the result of a statistical test to show that a result is probably not due to chance. In these cases, *significant* should not be used as a synonym for *important*.

E. Participle adjectives may present problems to some non-native speakers of English. Generally the *–ed* form indicates the result of an action or a finished state, whereas the *–ing* form is a cause or continuing state.

(30) The branches of a **developing** tree were highly successful in capturing light.

(31) The school has a **developed** social and cultural environment.

F. Adjectives can also be used as complements of linking verbs (1.7), rather than as part of a noun phrase.

(32) Structural changes in international commerce and finance **are necessary**.

Exercise 11: Vocabulary and Writing

Write a sentence adding your own ideas or content from your field. Use the words provided. Think carefully about the order and position of adjectives.

1. important / cultural _____

2. environmental / specific / concerns _____

3. common / political / issue _____

4. individual / different / preferences _____

5. results / promising _____

6. potentially / dangerous _____

5.8 Nominalization

A. **Nominalization** means changing a verb or other part of speech into a noun. This allows the writer to package an entire clause into one "thing" that can then be used as a subject or complement in a clause. Writers in many academic disciplines use this resource to pin down the phenomena they are studying as *facts* (Halliday & Martin, 1993, pp. 15–16). It also allows writers to avoid repeating explanations that the reader already knows. For example, since nominalization was defined in the first sentence of this paragraph, the term can be used rather than repeating *the process of changing a verb or other part of speech into a noun.*

> (33) Climate **change** is sometimes equated with global **warming,** but it involves much more than temperature **change.** The human activities that cause temperature **change** set in motion a series of associated phenomena: sea level **rise, loss** of polar sea ice, **melting** of continental glaciers, **changes** in **precipitation** patterns, progressive **shifting** in the habitats of species and the boundaries of ecosystems, **acidification** of the oceans, and more. These **changes** and impacts in turn create increasing risks to the planet's life **support** systems and to a myriad of species, including humankind.

B. There are five ways to form a nominalization (Hartnett, 1998).

1. Use the verb as a noun if possible (e.g., *plan, increase, change, experiment*). Likewise, some nouns have become accepted as verbs (e.g., *impact, influence*). Other verbs can function as nouns with a small spelling change (e.g., *to sell* → *a sale, to choose* → *a choice*).

2. Use the *–ing* form of the verb (e.g., *writing, teaching, bleeding*). This form is sometimes referred to as the **gerund.**

3. Add a suffix to the verb, such as *–al, –ance, –ion, –ation, –y, –ment* (e.g., *removal, compliance, erosion, modernization, mastery, measurement*).

4. Add a suffix to an adjective, such as *–ness, –ism,* or *–ity* (e.g., *appropriateness, activism, complexity*).

5. Add a suffix to another noun, which will change its meaning. Examples include *–ship, –hood,* and *–ism* (e.g., *leadership, adulthood, capitalism*).

It is also worth exploring synonyms; for example, a positive change could be described as an improvement, a development, an expansion, progress, or even an amelioration.

Exercise 12: Sentence Writing

Read each sentence. Write another sentence that begins with a nominalization of the underlined words.

> Example: Recently, researchers have <u>proposed</u> a new solution. *The proposal involves using social media to reach previously unstudied populations.*

1. The first step is to <u>analyze</u> the results. _____

   _____

2. Work on the new machine began to <u>move faster</u>. _____

   _____

3. It will be <u>difficult</u> to implement the policy. _____

   _____

4. Many tasks that were previously done by hand can now <u>be done on a computer</u>. _____

   _____

5. After extended use, the product <u>begins to lose quality</u>. _____

   _____

6. Researchers have <u>found</u> that many people only access the Internet on their smartphones.

   _____

7. Some public health experts <u>argue</u> that advertising of prescription drugs should be banned.

   _____

8. It is important for heads of research labs to <u>manage</u> their resources effectively. _____

   _____

Exercise 13: Sentence Revision

Rewrite these sentences from a human development textbook (Crain, 2000), changing the underlined words into nominalizations.

1. It is a worthy goal <u>to construct</u> such an integrative theory.

   _____

2. It <u>is very important</u> to the child who <u>is growing</u> to <u>acquire</u> speech.

   _____

3. When writing <u>was invented</u>, humans <u>achieved a lot</u>.

   _____

4. <u>The way that people regulate their words by themselves</u> helps us understand the way personality <u>develops</u> more broadly.

   _____

Exercise 14: Writing

Look at a piece of writing you have written recently. Highlight phrases that are currently clauses, verb phrases, or prepositional phrases that could be nominalized. Work with a partner to modify the sentences with nominalizations. Discuss the extent to which this improves your writing.

Grammar in Your Discipline

A. Look through several abstracts from journals in your discipline and find examples of:

1. descriptive adjectives

2. classifying adjectives

3. nominalization

4. double nouns

5. generic, indefinite, and definite references in noun phrases

B. Look again at your abstracts and answer these questions.

1. Is the title usually a sentence or a noun phrase? _____

2. What verb tenses are most common in the abstracts? If more than one tense is commonly used, is there a pattern in the usage? _____

3. Do writers use long or short noun phrases? _____

4. What kinds of modifiers and qualifiers are typical? _____

5. Do writers use nominalizations heavily? Do you notice any common phrases or patterns?

_____

C. Share your findings with a small group of writers from other disciplines. Do you notice any similarities or differences?

D. Write an abstract and title for a recent paper you have written or for one you are planning. If you are not writing at the moment, read a journal article and write an abstract for it, and then compare it to the published one. Pay close attention to noun phrases as you write and consider using nominalization to improve information flow. Edit your writing carefully for errors in noun phrase structure, articles, quantifiers, and subject-verb agreement.

For more information on abstracts, see Unit 8 of *Academic Writing for Graduate Students*, 3rd edition, and *Abstracts and the Writing of Abstracts* (Swales & Feak, 2009).

Hedging, Boosting, and Positioning

Throughout this book, grammar has been presented as expressing three levels of meanings: experiential (what happened), interpersonal (what you think about it), and textual (how it's organized). The three meanings operate simultaneously; for example, a writer's choice of verb tense tells the reader when the event happened, how the writer views it (relevant to the present, complete, unreal, ongoing, etc.), and how it connects to other events in surrounding sentences (1.8).

This unit focuses on interpersonal meaning, which is primarily created in academic writing through **hedging** and **boosting**. Hedges display "uncertainty, . . . deference, modesty, or respect for colleagues' views" (Hyland, 2000, p. 88). Boosters, on the other hand, show confidence in the author's claims and results. It is essential for graduate students, junior scholars, and experts to control their claims carefully throughout their professional writing and to "position" themselves appropriately in relation to other research and scholars.

There are many grammatical resources that allow writers to hedge, boost, and generally evaluate ideas, such as verb tenses, quantifiers, and connectors. Unit 6 focuses on areas of grammar that have not been introduced so far, primarily modal verbs, adverbs, conditionals, and comparatives.

> For more information on positioning, see Unit 1 of *Academic Writing for Graduate Students*, 3rd edition.

Since all grammar choices create interpersonal meanings along with experiential and textual meanings, one of the challenges in becoming an effective academic writer is learning to recognize and control the ways that words "encourage the readership to align" with your research, theories, and opinions (Hood, 2010, p. 38).

UNIT 6 Preview Test

Choose which sentence from each set has the stronger, more confident, or more positive meaning. Discuss your choices.

1. a. The result is somewhat surprising,
   b. The result is very surprising.

2. a. The research seems to support this view.
   b. The research is supportive of this view.

3. a. Technology is playing a more important role.
   b. Technology is playing a highly important role.

4. a. A number of physical housing features lead to unintentional injuries.
   b. A number of physical housing features may lead to unintentional injuries.
   c. A number of physical housing features may certainly lead to unintentional injuries.

5. a. Such improvements would allow scientists to examine organisms in nature in detail.
   b. Such improvements will allow scientists to examine organisms in nature in detail.

6. a. The results show that more needs to be done.
   b. The results suggest that more needs to be done.

Grammar Awareness: Data Commentary

Read the data commentary about enrollments of international students at U.S. universities. Complete the tasks.

Since at least the 1980s, the American educational system has attracted many students from all over the world. Data from the National Center for Education Statistics shows the increase of international students who want to enter U.S. institutes of higher education. Table B[1] shows the rate of change in the enrollment of international students as well as the total university and college population in the U.S. As can be seen from the data, the overall number of international students has increased exponentially in the last 60 years, although the rate of change has fluctuated wildly. The percentage of international students in U.S. universities decreased dramatically from 2002–2006. It is possible that the number of foreign students in that period was affected by a number of factors including the terrorist attacks of 2001, the SARS[2] outbreak in Asia, and the Japanese economic collapse. However, these factors did not appear to affect domestic enrollment. In fact, total higher education enrollment kept increasing that time, suggesting that more Americans were applying to colleges and universities. After 2006, new international student enrollment began to grow again at a rapid pace (over 15% between 2007 and 2008), but last year the pace slowed down considerably to only 1.2%. This decline is presumably caused by the current recession because previous economic downturns also correlated with similar drops. However, the total number of foreign students in the U.S. is very likely to continue growing.

1. Which words and phrases show the writers' confidence in their interpretations?

   _____

2. Which words and phrases show uncertainty in the writers' interpretations?

   _____

3. Who do you think the writers are? How much expertise do you think they have? Why?

   _____

---

[1] The table can be found on the Institute for International Education's website, www.iie.org.

[2] SARS = Severe Acute Respiratory Syndrome

6.1 Modal Verbs

A. **Modal verbs** are an important language tool to hedge or boost. A modal is an auxiliary verb that can fill the finite verb slot and is always followed by a verb in the base (infinitive) form. Table 6.1 lists the most common modals in academic writing.

Table 6.1 Common Modal Verbs in Academic Writing	
Hedging (Softening Claims)	**Boosting (Strengthening Claims)**
may (not), might (not), can, could, should (= possibility, prediction) *should* (= hedged recommendation) *would* (see 6.2)	*will* (= strong prediction) *must* (= high certainty; or a very strong obligation) *can* (= ability: definitely able to do something) *cannot* (= will certainly not)

Adapted from Biber et al., 1999.

B. The most frequently used modal for hedging in writing is *may*. There is very little difference in meaning between *can, could, may,* and *might* when they are used to hedge a claim or prediction. *Should* is less common with this function, but when used, it sounds very uncertain.

> (1a) Iterations in temperature **may mean** greater variability in annual climatic events.
>
> (1b) Iterations in temperature **mean/will mean** greater variability in annual climatic events.
>
> (1c) Iterations in temperature **should mean** greater variability in annual climatic events.

Sentence 1a is the writer's original choice, Sentence 1b sounds much stronger, and Sentence 1c is somewhat weaker.

C. *Should* is also used to hedge a recommendation (by contrast with the stronger modal verb *must*, which is less commonly used in academic writing). This may be useful in the implications or conclusion section of a paper or in a shorter text such as a data commentary.

> (2) From a humanitarian standpoint, the United States government **should** invest resources in controlling the global spread of malaria.

Should also appears in MICUSP to introduce a hypothesis or research question (Sentence 3).

> (3) If the two species are segregating spatially, they **should be found** in different proportions and different relative abundances in the three habitats.

D. *Can* is both a hedging and boosting word, and statistically it is the most common modal verb overall in academic writing. However, *can* is often used to indicate ability rather than possibility or certainty. When *can* is used to hedge or boost, adverbs clarify the meaning:

> (4) Credible guidelines **can certainly** be established. [boosting]

> (5) These findings **can possibly** be explained by earlier research. [hedging]

E. Modals can be used in the passive voice. The infinitive of *be* + the past participle is used to form the passive after a modal verb. Note that a *by* phrase is possible, especially when it describes a process using an *–ing* non-finite clause.

> For more information on the use of the passive in descriptions of processes, see Unit 3 (pages 119–125) of *Academic Writing for Graduate Students,* 3rd edition.

> (6) This can **be achieved by allowing** the students to use a task-oriented approach.

> (7) Lesions in the cornea **could be caused by physical damage**.

F. Although it is not usually possible to add tense to a modal verb, the main verb that follows can be in perfect or progressive aspect, but these forms are quite rare.

> (8) The duration of the interventions **may have contributed** to these findings. [perfect aspect]

> (9) CO_2 and some other gases **may be changing** our climate. [progressive aspect]

G. The negatives of some modal verbs do not have the same strength as the affirmative (positive) forms. *Cannot* is much stronger than *can*; it means something is certainly impossible or must absolutely not be allowed. *Have to* is similar to *must* in strength, but its negative form, *do not have to*, means something is permitted or possible but not necessary.

> (10) The students were informed that they **did not have to** participate in the study.

Exercise 1: Sentence Completion

Choose the best words to complete the sentences. Discuss your choices.

1. Symptoms of malaria usually resemble the flu; however, in young children, pregnant women, and immuno-compromised patients the disease (will / may) lead to eventual death.

2. Future research (must / should) check whether individuals can actually learn to perform this injury avoidance maneuver in a real sideways fall.

3. A focus on proficiency standards might (be seen / see) as a political statement about the value of education for all students.

4. We hypothesize that the results (can / should) be very similar because both techniques have the same effect.

5. Different test environments such as temperature and humidity could (have contributed / be contributing) to the different results between two papers.

6. This problem can be resolved (changing / by changing) the shape of the mid-rail from square to rectangular.

Exercise 2: Grammatical Awareness

Choose the sentence in each set that has the strongest claim (that is, does the most boosting or least hedging).

1. a. Community gardens can improve mental health.

   b. Community gardens might improve mental health.

2. a. In order for this outcome to occur, the United Nations must take the initiative.

   b. In order for this outcome to occur, the United Nations should take the initiative.

3. a. Not learning to read as a third grader will certainly have an effect on school achievement.

   b. Not learning to read as a third grader can have an effect on your later school achievement.

4. a. Thus, historical precedence cannot always be generalized and applied to foreign problems.

   b. Thus, historical precedence cannot be generalized and applied to foreign problems.

5. a. When humans misread the symbols of other members of their species, violence can result.

   b. When humans misread the symbols of other members of their species, violence results.

6. a. One improvement is that women who are now allowed to compete for jobs can support their families in the same manner as men.

   b. One improvement is that women who are now allowed to compete for jobs may be able to support their families in the same manner as men.

7. a. Therefore, it is also important to examine the age evolution of the attitudes toward unhappy marriages.

   b. Therefore, it has to also be important to examine the age evolution of the attitudes toward unhappy marriages.

8. a. A tool such as this cannot reflect the same findings if used in a general population of asthmatic children.

   b. A tool such as this might not reflect the same findings if used in a general population of asthmatic children.

Exercise 3: Writing

Choose a problem in your field of study or in current events. Write answers to these questions using modal verbs to hedge and boost where appropriate.

1. What might have caused this problem? _____

   _____

2. What may be happening now as a result of this problem? _____

   _____

3. How should it be solved? _____

   _____

4. Might that solution actually work? _____

   _____

6.2 *Would*

A. *Would* is used for a prediction or hypothesis about events or states that might happen in the future but are not currently real or possible (Biber et al., 1999, p. 496). *Would* is considered a hedging device because it has an unreal meaning that distances the writer from the claim.

(11) To tackle this challenge **would require** at least three things. [No one is tackling the challenge now, but if someone did, it would require three things.]

(12) These educational programs **would be** preventive in that active participation **would help** thwart future problems in these areas. [The programs do not yet exist.]

B. *Would* is used in **unreal conditional** (*if*) clauses (6.4). However, in academic writing the *if* clause is often implicit; that is, we understand there is a condition, but it is not directly stated.

(13) Most people **would agree** that the ideal educational system **would properly educate** everyone. [The condition *if they were asked* is not stated, but the writer doesn't have data from an actual survey to back up the claim.]

C. Be careful to distinguish between *would like* and *prefer*. *Would like* can either refer to an unfulfilled wish or to a present desire (a more polite, and therefore hedged, version of *I want*). On the other hand, *prefer* refers to a preference for an activity that already takes place.

(14) Exactly 79.3 percent of respondents said they **would like** to know more about the human-animal bond.

(15) Some students **prefer** to study in total silence; others **prefer** to study listening to soft music.

Exercise 4: Sentence Completion

Complete these sentences with *would, would like,* or *will*. More than one choice may be possible. Discuss your choices.

1. The outcome is less certain under the government's proposal. The results _____ probably be positive for small health centers.

2. The new rules _____ require businesses to provide more detailed forecasts.

3. Human-induced climate change _____ continue for many decades.

4. The evidence suggests that oil _____ become more scarce and expensive.

5. The agreement should be used as a model by states who _____ to work together.

6. In any future study, a wider range of participants _____ certainly improve the generalizability of the results.

6.3 Adverbs

A. The strength of any verb, including a modal verb, can be hedged or boosted with an adverb. Adverbs cannot be described simply as hedging or boosting; they can be placed on a scale of confidence (Hood, 2010). For example, *frequently* can be a hedge if it means "less than always" but a booster if it means "often."

B. Most hedging and boosting adverbs in academic writing appear in the middle of the clause they modify (Biber et al., 1999, p. 872). Their exact position depends on the verb. There are three places they appear:

For more information, see page 105 of *Academic Writing for Graduate Students,* 3rd edition.

1. **before** the main verb when it is also the finite verb: *The results <u>apparently</u> show. . . .*
2. **between** the finite and the main verb: *This has been <u>somewhat</u> validated by. . . .*
3. **after** *be* as a main verb: *This is <u>presumably</u> why. . . .*

Adverbs can be moved to the start of the clause, which gives them greater weight. Adverbs can also be used in front of adjectives or quantifiers, but not nouns (1.3).

(16) Outbreaks of these diseases are **relatively common**.

(17) **Only a few** texts address issues of discrimination.

(18a) INCORRECT: A **frequently** complaint is . . . .

(18b) CORRECT: A **frequently heard** complaint is . . . .

(18c) CORRECT: A **frequent** complaint is . . . .

C. Many common adverbs of frequency and possibility are used as hedges or boosters in academic writing, as shown in Table 6.2 (Hinkel, 2004):

Table 6.2 Common Adverbs of Frequency and Possibility	
frequently, often	generally, in general, usually, normally
largely, typically	sometimes, at times, partially
most of the time, on many/numerous occasions	in most cases, in this/that case
almost never, rarely, seldom, hardly ever	almost/nearly always, invariably
possibly, perhaps, probably, likely, unlikely	

Based on Hinkel, 2004, p. 316ff.

D. Some other hedging adverbs are far more common in academic writing than other forms of English, such as *presumably* (something is probably true but not proven), *theoretically* (something could possibly exist or take place, but it is unlikely), and *somewhat* (which makes clauses less strong or shocking).

(19) The life cycle of most fish in the delta is **presumably** similar to that of the few well-studied species.

(20) **Theoretically**, putting all these engineering heads together should produce the best design possible.

(21) This is **somewhat** surprising given the autobiographical as well as cinematic importance of this topic.

E. Adverbs such as *naturally, of course, obviously, always, never,* and *ever* typically have a boosting effect, and occur fairly frequently in professional academic writing. According to MICUSP, graduate student writing uses boosters but not very frequently. There are also differences among disciplines—for example, *of course* occurs almost exclusively in the humanities and very rarely in science and engineering texts (Davies, 2011).

(22) This did not mean, **of course**, that Italian immigrants were free from the effects of prejudice. [graduate history paper]

F. Some other common adverbs used to boost a claim include *actually* (a possibility that the reader might not expect), *indeed* (which generally boosts a hedged statement by showing that an idea is true even though it had been doubted), *easily, especially, particularly,* and *significantly.*

(23) The expectation of reward **can actually** undermine intrinsic motivation and creativity of performance.

(24) This fascination with gold **can easily** be explained by its radiance and glitter.

(25) Part of the answer **may indeed** lie in our genes.

(26) Because of past and future anthropogenic emissions of CO_2, the climate **may** depart **significantly** from its natural course over the next 50,000 years.

Note the combination of a hedging modal (*may*) and a boosting adverb (*significantly*) in Sentence 26, a common tactic for academic writers to show confidence but leave some room for error.

Exercise 5: Sentence Revision

Change the strength of these claims by hedging in Sentences 1–5 and boosting in Sentences 6–10 using adverbs, modals, and other techniques.

1. Machines will replace humans for dangerous and repetitive tasks.

2. There is no doubt that humanity will be in danger when computers are able to think for themselves.

3. Recent technological advances have all been for entertainment not life enhancement.

4. Smartphones have brought no benefits, only distractions.

5. Because children watch more TV and have more access to the Internet, they are growing up to be antisocial and violent.

6. Machines are useful for improving productivity.

7. Technology may perhaps be prevented from threatening human existence.

8. Increased access to information means that people might make better choices.

9. Internet searching is relatively efficient in some situations.

10. Many inventions have improved our quality of life.

Exercise 6: Vocabulary and Writing

Will English continue to be the international language of science, academia, and business, or could other languages (for example, Chinese, Arabic, or Spanish) take over this role? Write at least three sentences with confident (boosted) predictions and at least three sentences with less certain (hedged) guesses about the future.

boosting

_____

_____

_____

hedging

_____

_____

_____

6.4 Conditionals

A. **Conditional clauses** are subordinate clauses that usually start with _if._ Less often they start with _when_ or _unless._ Conditionals hedge because they show that a claim is true _if_ some condition is met. There are three types of conditionals: one real and two unreal forms. **Real conditionals** are used for conditions that have happened, will happen, or always happen. The first unreal form, the hypothetical, describes conditions that might exist in the future. The other unreal conditional, the counterfactual, describes conditions that might have existed in the past.

B. Table 6.3 summarizes the most common tense choices in conditional clauses. Most combinations of tenses within the real or unreal rows are possible, but it is not usually acceptable to mix real and unreal clauses in the same sentence. The _if_ clause can be used before or after the main clause (2.2).

Table 6.3 Verb Tenses with Conditional Clauses		
	_if_ **(Condition) Clause**	**Main (Results) Clause**
Real Conditional	present simple, present progressive, past simple, past progressive, _be going to_	any appropriate past or present tense or future form (especially _will_), plus modal verbs
Unreal Conditional	past simple* past perfect	_would/could/might_ + verb _would/could/might have_ + past participle

*_were_ is used for singular and plural nouns and pronouns.

C. Most style guides discourage using *will* and *would* in the *if* clause, although spoken English permits them.

> (27a) CORRECT: If this change **occurs**, long-term environmental protection may result.
>
> (27b) INCORRECT: If this change **will occur** . . . .
>
> (28a) CORRECT: Even if the engine **failed**, the rotor would continue to turn.
>
> (28b) INCORRECT: Even if the engine **would fail** . . . .

D. One common use of conditionals in academic writing is to explain a situation (real or hypothetical) that would make a claim true (Carter-Thomas & Rowley-Jolivet, 2008).

> (29) Old deep water **can** be removed relatively easily **if** it **is** transported southward. [real conditional, present or future meaning]
>
> (30) **If** our planet **faced** the same direction as it revolves around the sun, we **would have** six months of daylight and a six-month summer. [unreal conditional]
>
> (31) For example, **if** a child **breaks** a window, it **makes** sense to punish him or her with clean-up responsibilities. [real conditional, general rule]
>
> (32) **If** the stock **went** down, the customer **lost**. [real conditional, past time]

E. Conditionals also hedge claims by introducing restrictions that may make the statement true or false. This may be done with a full or reduced clause.

> (33) **If** this **is true**, pesticide use could increase susceptibility to intestinal parasites, hepatitis, malaria, and respiratory infections.
>
> (34) The superstring Theory of Everything, **if discovered**, would be yet another so-called law of the universe.

A reduced clause is only possible if the omitted subject of the *if* clause matches the subject of the main clause. For example, in Sentence 34, the implied subject of *discovered* is *the superstring Theory of Everything*. However, in Sentence 33, *this* refers to the previous sentence and not to *pesticide use*, so reducing the clause to *if true* would be ambiguous.

F. The final function of the conditional is as a concessive. A concessive sentence describes two opposite points of view, without saying that either is completely wrong (Warchał, 2010). Usually, this involves acknowledging that a limitation exists with the writer's claim, but that claim is still basically true. This meaning may be expressed with *even if*, *although*, or *if* + (not) + adjective or adverb.

> For more information about how unreal conditionals can be used to hedge criticisms, see Unit 6 of *Academic Writing for Graduate Students*, 3rd edition.

(35) The sanctions, in practice **if not** intent, contributed to a shortage of printing material.

(36) **Even if** such studies prove to be of minor educational significance, they may still have scientific importance.

Exercise 7: Grammatical Judgment

Read each sentence. Mark C if it is grammatically correct and appropriate for formal academic writing. Mark I if it is incorrect. Correct the sentences marked I.

1.   C / I   Television soap operas are interesting, even they mainly serve to distract audiences from their real lives.

2.   C / I   If people were willing to spontaneously cooperate, everyone would profit.

3.   C / I   It would be desirable if students would be able to move through college faster.

4.   C / I   This were to occur, major businesses would quietly leave the country.

5.   C / I   It would have been helpful if there were better training in this area.

6.   C / I   They would never have entered into the transaction if they had known they were giving up their home.

7.   C / I   Most patients had more damage if treatment was delayed.

8.   C / I   Classroom sizes should be minimized if is possible.

Exercise 8: Sentence Completion

Complete these conditional sentences with your own ideas.

1. If technology is used responsibly, _____.

2. If hospitals did not have access to medical technology, _____.

3. If robots replaced teachers, _____.

4. Before cell phones, if an emergency happened on campus, _____.

5. Even if some machines are only designed for entertainment, _____.

6. If made available for ordinary customers, _____.

7. If true, _____.

8. If the warnings of climate scientists are accepted, _____.

Exercise 9: Writing

The host of a public radio talk show devoted to science might ask his guests, "What would you do with unlimited funding?" Imagine you could conduct any research study without regard to cost or other practical matters. Write a paragraph or a personal essay in response to this question.

If you are not a researcher, what changes would you make in your profession or workplace if money were no object?

6.5 Comparatives, Superlatives, and Equatives

A. **Comparatives** (*bigger, more/less important*), superlatives (*biggest, most/least important*), and equatives (*as important as*) express how similar or different an item (word, idea, action, or state) is to another item or items. These structures can both hedge or boost: a technique may be *more reliable* than another (boosting), but a *more reliable* technique is also hedged in comparison to a *very reliable* technique (Hood, 2010). Similarly, **superlatives** tend to be boosters, but the *most reliable* test available might still not actually be very reliable.

(37) The results would have been **more reliable** if the researchers had double-checked their findings with the participants.

(38) **Better** economies will increase household spending or purchasing power.

(39) One of **the most important goals** of epidemiology is to avoid the occurrence of pandemics.

B. Only adjectives that are **gradable** have a comparative form. Gradable means that the adjective can have different levels of intensity, for example, from *somewhat* acceptable to *very* acceptable. Non-gradable adjectives are **binary** in meaning and do not allow intensifying adverbs, comparatives, or superlatives. For example, a person may be *unemployed* but not *very unemployed* or *more unemployed*—you either have a job or you don't. Other examples include *continuous, countless, simultaneous, virtual, unique,* and *stationary.* Classifying adjectives (5.7) are almost never gradable.

C. Adverbs can also be used in comparative and superlative forms by adding *more* or *most. More* and *most* can also be used as quantifiers in a noun phrase with a similar effect. *More* and *most* can be considered the comparative and superlative forms of *some.*

> (40) International students who have a strong social support system tend to adjust to college life in the United States **more quickly and effectively** than those who do not.
>
> (41) Though many other factors enter into the debate, these are the ones that received **the most attention** in 1990.

D. Adjectives and adverbs can be downgraded by using *less* (comparative) and *the least* (superlative).

> (42) Heart disease is **less frequent** among those regularly engaged in heavy labor.
>
> (43) The projections indicate that coal will remain among **the least expensive** fuel sources.
>
> (44) Items located toward the middle of a sequence are recalled **less easily**.

E. Comparative clauses and phrases allow writers to name the "basis of the comparison," that is, what the item is being compared to (Biber et al., 1999, p. 536).

> (45) The group claims that trolley service is **more** reliable, **more** comfortable, and **less** costly **than bus service**. [the noun phrase with *bus service* is the basis of comparison]
>
> (46) Women are commonly viewed as **more** accepting of others **than men are**. [the clause *how men are viewed* is the basis of comparison]

The use of *than* is another form of hedging. In Sentence 45, for example, the writer only claims that trolleys are more reliable than buses and not, for example, cars or airplanes.

F. **Equative** phrases and clauses show what an item is *the same as* or *similar to*. Notice the use of the definite article with *the same*. Equative phrases and clauses also use the structure *as* + adjective/adverb + *as*.

> (47) Climate information for **the same period** might be used to complement this dataset.

> (48) Communication skills have become **as important as** technical discipline-based skills.

> (49) Physical proximity to live music is not **as important as** it once was. [finite clause]

> (50) Academic cheating may be **as simple as** using crib notes in class or plagiarizing others in written assignments. [non-finite –*ing* clause]

Exercise 10: Sentence Writing

Write a paragraph about the data in Table 6.4 using comparative and equative structures.

Table 6.4 "How did you secure your most recent job?"			
Job Search Tool	Generation X (age 18–29)	Generation Y (age 30–47)	Baby Boomers (age 48–65)
Online job board	31%	24%	19%
Word of mouth	22%	23%	22%
Direct approach from employer	16%	18%	19%
Print ad	4%	8%	10%
Social media	1%	1%	1%
Other	8%	10%	13%

Kelly Global Workforce Index, 2011, retrieved from http://media.marketwire.com/.

6.6 Evaluative Language

A. Word choice expresses a great deal about a writer's stance, attitudes, and confidence. Very few language choices are completely neutral in terms of interpersonal meaning, so effective writers choose words carefully to establish their own authority and align the reader with their ideas. Sentence 51 begins a university press release describing new economic research.

> (51) To generate income, **communities** should think outside the
> **big box** of large **corporations** and concentrate on **small**, locally
> owned businesses and **startups**.

The subject in Sentence 51 is *communities* (not *towns, cities,* or *municipalities*), which has the positive meaning of people who do not just live together but have a connection. *Big box* is a pun on the phrase "think out of the box," but the phrase *big-box stores* has a more negative, impersonal, unfriendly feel than *major retailers* or *discount superstores*. In this sentence, *small* clearly has a positive meaning by contrast with *big box*, and *startups* perhaps appeal to the reader's shared value in entrepreneurship; the writer did not choose *inexperienced store owners* or *struggling new companies*.

> For more information on "scare quotes," a technique that can show a negative attitude to any word, see pages 274–275 of *Academic Writing for Graduate Students*, 3rd edition.

B. Reporting verbs can be evaluative or neutral. Evaluative verbs either show support for or distance from the noun clause. Celce-Murcia and Larsen-Freeman (1999) classify verbs as having the basic meanings of *know* (relating to facts and so neutral) and *believe* (evaluative, relating to opinions), leading to the different shades of meaning shown in Table 6.5.

Table 6.5 Evaluation with Reporting Verbs	
Evaluative (*believe*)	**Neutral (*know*)**
prove, demonstrate, confirm, establish [know + give reasons]	*reveal, show, point out, explain, say, write, observe, indicate, state, report, note* [know + make public]
admit, recognize, acknowledge [say something you perhaps didn't want to]	*realize, notice, find, conclude, determine* [come to know]
claim [say something that's not obvious or perhaps not true]	*discover, reveal* [make known something that isn't obvious]
deny [refuse to accept]	*imply* [draw a conclusion that is not explicitly made]
argue, contend, insist [say something not obvious, but give reasons]	*propose, hypothesize, estimate* [true based on known conditions]
assume, assert, maintain [make public without giving reasons]	
suspect, suggest, speculate [believe, but not fully confidently]	
doubt [think something is **not** true]	
be certain [believe without a doubt]	
emphasize, stress [know or believe with confidence]	
recommend [want others to believe]	

Adapted and expanded from Celce-Murcia & Larsen-Freeman, 1999, p. 703.

C. Action verbs can also carry evaluations. For example, *try* suggests an incomplete attempt to do something (negative evaluation), while *succeed, achieve,* and *complete* are more positive. On the other end of the scale are highly negative verbs such as *fail, collapse, neglect,* and *diminish,* all of which are fairly frequent in published academic writing.

> (52) The school **attempts** to provide students with programs that allow a cultural understanding across different social classes. [The writer goes on to show how the school fails in its attempts.]
>
> (53) The novel **succeeds** in creating a compelling and imaginative new perspective from which to contemplate human history.
>
> (54) This paper **attempts** to characterize the optimal audit mechanism.

The use of *attempts* in Sentence 54 is common in MICUSP. In this example, the writer is hedging the paper's purpose. This may be because the writer is uncertain whether the best possible audit mechanism has been characterized. The writer might be concerned about the level of expertise and authority needed to claim anything stronger. Interestingly, even verbs of completion are often hedged with modal verbs in MICUSP, perhaps for the same reasons.

> (55) The proposed plan **can accomplish** the same goal.

D. Descriptive adjectives (5.7) can be used to hedge or boost. For example:

---

boosting: *confident, sure, certain, clear, positive, effective, true, firm, constant, accurate, solid, reliable, robust, definite, trustworthy, dependable, unquestionable, valid*

hedging: *uncertain, ambiguous, unclear, vague, tentative, doubtful, hesitant, exploratory, cautious, speculative, provisional, preliminary, unconfirmed, so-called*

> (56) The long-term result must remain **speculative.**
>
> (57) The current findings support a **cautious** approach.
>
> (58) This article is an attempt to clarify the situation with **accurate, up-to-date** facts and figures.

For more information on how evaluative adjectives are used differently across disciplines, see pages 262–265 of *Academic Writing for Graduate Students,* 3rd edition.

E. The linking verbs *seem* and *appear* can be used to hedge, but they can also be combined with boosting adjectives to express reasonable but not excessive confidence.

> (59) This **seems** like a **reliable** prediction.
>
> (60) It **appears** to be **especially true** for girls who **seem** to be **particularly** at risk.

These verbs can also be used in the noun phrase as adjectives (*seeming, apparent*) or more commonly as adverbs modifying adjectives (*seemingly, apparently*).

F. Very often, writers have a choice between a more neutral noun, verb, or adjective, and one that hedges or boosts the meaning, making it more positive or negative. For example, the birth rate could *grow* (neutral), *explode* (strongly positive), *collapse* (strongly negative), or *creep up* (positive, but hedged). An experiment can be described as a *breakthrough* (strongly positive) or a *setback* (strongly negative).

Exercise 11: Vocabulary Analysis

Choose the word in parentheses that is the stronger evaluative word in each sentence, and circle the type of evaluation, positive (+) or negative (-). Discuss your choices. (Note that at least one word in each pair appears on the Academic Word List of commonly used general academic vsocabulary; Coxhead, 2000.)

1. + / -   These factors have been identified as potentially contributing to this (preference / bias).

2. + / -   It is time for the nation to adopt a (comprehensive / specific) plan to dramatically reduce smoking.

3. + / -   Technology can also be used in ways that (distort / change) and misrepresent the public pulse.

4. + / -   People in the richest nations are (reluctant / unwilling) to sacrifice economic growth.

5. + / -   Even inexperienced hackers can probe computer networks for weaknesses and (use / exploit) any security holes they find.

6. + / -   A(n) (brief / inadequate) written survey was given to sport spectators.

7. + / -   Such a limiting content-based ban (violates / breaks) the First Amendment.

8. + / -   Most experts expect a (revolution / development) in the power and energy industries over the next few decades.

Exercise 12: Language Analysis

These paragraphs are taken from a report published by the Institute of International Education, a nonprofit organization that promotes "the international exchange of people and ideas." This report, *What International Students Think about U.S. Higher Education* (Chow, 2011), was prepared in collaboration with Education USA, an organization that "actively promote[s] U.S. higher education around the world." Keep this in mind as you complete the activity.

A. Underline all the evaluative language in this paragraph and discuss its effects with a partner.

In 2009/10, the U.S. hosted a record high of over 690,000 international students (Open Doors, 2010). Although the U.S. market share has declined in the last decade, the U.S. nevertheless hosted far more international students than any other destination. The United Kingdom, the second most popular international study destination, hosted about 450,000 international students, two-thirds of the U.S. total.

B. Discuss the effect that the different lexical choices in square brackets would have on the text. Which do you think was in the original paragraph?

According to UNESCO, in 2008, the top five study destinations (the U.S., the U.K., France, Australia and Germany) hosted 55 percent of the world's tertiary-level mobile students. At less than four percent, the proportion of international students to overall higher education enrollment in the U.S. remains ❶ [quite small / almost insignificant / unacceptably low] compared to other top host countries, ❷ [although / and / while] the percentage is higher at the graduate level (11 percent). Furthermore, in 2009–2010, ❸ [fewer than two thirds / more than 62 percent / more than half] of international students in the U.S. were hosted at fewer than 200 colleges and universities. With ❹ [more than 4,000 / many / thousands of] institutions of higher education in the United States, there is ❺ [some possibility / tremendous potential / little chance] for more institutions to host more international students, ❻ [perhaps / only / particularly] at the undergraduate and non-degree levels.

Grammar in Your Discipline

A. Look through one or more data commentaries in your discipline (for example, from the Results and/or Discussion sections of a journal article or from a professional business or research report) and find examples of the following:

1. modal verbs used to hedge results

2. modal verbs used to boost findings

3. adverbs used for hedging or boosting

4. conditional clauses used for hedging or boosting

5. other words and phrases that evaluate claims, ideas, and opinions

B. Look again at your data commentaries and answer these questions.

1. Which is more frequent: hedging or boosting? Why? _____

2. Do writers combine hedging and boosting techniques? How? _____

3. Which tenses are used with conditional clauses? Why? _____

C. Share your findings with a small group of writers from other disciplines. Do you notice any similarities or differences?

D. Write a commentary on a set of data that is of interest, importance, or controversy in your field. Pay close attention to hedging and boosting as you write. Edit your writing carefully for errors in modal verbs, word choice, and conditional clauses.

For more information on writing data commentaries, see Unit 4 of *Academic Writing for Graduate Students*, 3rd edition, which also includes a further discussion of hedging and boosting.

Collocation and Corpus Searching

According to British linguist J. R. Firth, "You shall know a word by the company it keeps." One of the keys to successful academic writing is to put the right words together. This is called **collocation**: the tendency of certain words to occur together. Sometimes, a good combination will simply sound right; at other times, though, you will need help choosing the best phrase. The unit explores different types of collocations and online tools for finding them.

Unit 7 Preview Test

Complete the sentences with a natural collocation. Don't worry if you don't know the best collocation; choose a word that makes sense.

1. Students and their teachers come to the library media center to _____ research for class projects.

2. This analysis provides _____ evidence that the present model represents a robust description of the data.

3. This article _____ the issue of overpopulation.

4. The distance-learning format can present some new challenges _____ instructors.

5. Many times these sources of data are at odds, _____ providing fuel for class discussion.

Grammar Awareness: Essay

Read the introduction to an argumentative essay submitted for a graduate psychology course (included in MICUSP). Then complete the tasks.

Dissatisfactions with Job Satisfaction Measurement:
The Context-Dependency of Work Attitudes

Job satisfaction is the most ❶ extensively studied variable in organizational behavior research (Spector, 1997). According to Roznowski and Hulin (1992), an employee's job satisfaction is the single most important ❷ piece of information that managers can have in order to predict outcomes that ❸ matter to the organization, including turnover, absenteeism, and performance (Spector, 1997). Recently, Weiss (2002) criticized the job satisfaction literature for overlooking advances in social psychology about the nature and processes of judgments and attitudes. He proposed a reconceptualization of the construct of job satisfaction according to these advances, and defined job satisfaction as an "evaluative judgment . . . about one's job or job situation" (Weiss, 2002. p. 175).

We believe that ❹ advances in social psychology have important implications for the measurement, as well as conceptualization, of job satisfaction. ❺ We begin by summarizing a series of controversies and ❻ unresolved questions in job satisfaction research. Next, ❼ drawing on the social cognition, judgment, and life satisfaction literatures, ❽ we illustrate how satisfaction measures are ❾ heavily dependent on context. We discuss how the questions themselves can shape satisfaction judgments, and then examine how ❿ the larger context in which these questions are asked can shape satisfaction judgments. Throughout this discussion, we present data to illustrate these points. We conclude with an agenda for ⓫ future research to both document and account for context effects on satisfaction.

1. Complete the sentences using words from the underlined collocations in the essay.

   a. This paper begins _____ the previous literature on school reform.

   b. Thanks to _____ technology, it is now possible to recover information even from shredded documents.

   c. The study provides a key _____ about the behavior of this protein.

   d. The authors drew _____ their experience in government.

   e. The economy is _____ dependent on the housing market for growth.

2. Finish these sentences, which contain some of the underlined collocations in the essay, with your own ideas.

a. _____ has/have been extensively studied.

b. _____ matter/matters to experts in the field of _____.

c. One of the most important unresolved questions in _____ is

_____ .

d. This paper illustrates how _____ .

e. The larger context in which _____ affects

_____ .

f. Future research is needed _____ .

7.1 Writing with a Corpus

A. One way to investigate **collocations** is by using a corpus. A **corpus** is a large electronic collection of texts that you can search to learn about typical patterns in a particular type of discourse, such as academic writing.

B. The easiest corpus to use is the internet. If you are not sure whether a phrase is commonly used, a search on your favorite search engine will find example sentences or reveal that there are few hits. However, not all writing on the Internet is necessarily a good model and far less of it is academic. One solution is to limit your search to university and U.S. government websites. In Google, you simply add this string to the end of your search term: site:.edu, .gov.

You can also search Google Scholar (www.scholar.google.com), which will find examples of the phrase in academic books and articles. You may not be able to view the complete articles, however, unless you are on the network of a university that subscribes to the journal.

C. The Michigan Corpus of Upper-level Students Papers (MICUSP) contains graduate-level writing that received A grades at the University of Michigan (www.elicorpora.info/). Many examples and exercises in this textbook were drawn from MICUSP. You can search for individual words and phrases to see how other graduate students have used them.

D. The Corpus of Contemporary American English (COCA) is a massive corpus of texts (more than 425 million words) from 1990 to the present. COCA allows very sophisticated searches, and its "five-minute guided tour" is highly recommended. The website is www.americancorpus.org, and the corpus is maintained by Professor Mark Davies at Brigham Young University. Free registration is required after a certain number of searches.

E. Professor Davies has designed an alternative interface to COCA that focuses exclusively on academic writing: www.wordandphrase.info/academic. This site offers definitions, collocations, synonyms, and example sentences for the most common 60,000 words in academic written English. It also usefully provides information about the ranking of each word and its relative frequency in different disciplines.

Exercise 1: Searching the Internet

Go to www.google.com and run these searches to answer the questions.

1. Which is more frequently used: different *from* or different *than*?

                                                    # of results

   "different from" site:.edu, .gov   _____

   "different than" site:.edu, .gov   _____

   (The quotation marks tell Google to look for the words together.)

2. Is the phrase *a bunch of* common in academic writing? Search www.scholar.google.com for "a bunch of" (in quotation marks), and compare the number of results to phrases such as "a lot of" or "a number of." Repeat the search on MICUSP. Complete the chart. What can you conclude about these phrases?

	Google	MICUSP
a bunch of		
a lot of		
a number of		

3. Search Google Scholar (or Google, adding site:.edu, .gov to your search term) for the phrase "further research is needed." Based on your results, do you think it would be considered plagiarism to use this clause in your own writing? Repeat the search with other phrases you have read frequently in your field.

   _____

   _____

Exercise 2: Searching MICUSP

Go to MICUSP or another corpus academic writing. Conduct searches to answer the questions.

1. Many non-native speakers find the word *actually* difficult to use. Search for it on MICUSP: What advice would you give to a writer who asked you how to use this word?

   _____

   _____

2. What verb tense is used in your field after the phrase *the purpose of this study*? Search for the phrase, and compare with *the purpose of this paper*. Share your findings with a classmate from a different field, if possible.

   _____

   _____

Exercise 3: Searching COCA

Access COCA at www.americancorpus.org. If you haven't created a free account yet, now would be a good time to do so.

1. Imagine you have read the phrase *in the absence of* in a paper. Is this a useful phrase for academic writing? Type the phrase in the search box marked *Word(s)* (no quotation marks), and select *Chart* in the *Display* box above it.

   _____

   _____

2. What prepositions are used with evidence? Type "evidence" in the search box, and then click on POS List. POS means Part of Speech. Choose prep.ALL (all prepositions). This should insert the code "[i*]" after the word *evidence*. Now, select List in the Display box and choose the Academic section. Look at the list of prepositions; click on the top two or three, and you will see example sentences. What do you notice?

   _____

   _____

3. Is the noun *research* countable in American English? That is, can you write about many researches? Enter "researches" in the search box, choose Chart display and the Academic section. If you run the search now, COCA will return results for the verb researches (*he researches*) as well as plural nouns. To limit the search to nouns, type a period after "researches" and then select noun.ALL from the POS List. The full search term is researches.[nn*]. Make sure there is no space between the period and the square brackets. Run the search. The results are given as frequency and as words per million, that is, how often your phrase occurs in a million words of academic writing. What do you notice?

_____

_____

Exercise 4: Searching WordAndPhrase.Info

Go to www.wordandphrase.info/academic, which shares the same login as COCA. Click on Academic Vocabulary List. The short guided tour is recommended for new users.

1. What information can you find about the use of *evidence* in academic writing? Enter *evidence* in the Word box, and choose to include both technical and non-academic words. Click Search. Look at the frequency information your screen.

   a. Is the noun or verb more common?

   _____

   b. The ratio tells you whether a word is more common in academic writing than other types of English. For example, a ratio of 1.50 means that the word occurs 50 percent more often in academic writing. What does the ratio information tell you about the use of the verb *evidence*?

   _____

   c. Click on the verb entry for *evidence*. Skim through the sample sentences that appear. What do you notice about the grammatical form of the verb?

   _____

   d. In which disciplines is the verb *evidence* most common? Is this a verb you might need in your academic or professional writing?

   _____

   e. Look at the noun entry for *evidence*. Which verb and adjectives collocate most strongly with evidence?

   _____

2. Imagine that you are writing a paper, and you realize you have repeated the word *problem* too many times. Change to the non-academic version of the site by clicking use all genres. Search for *problem*, and look at the synonyms. Click on a few to see sample sentences, and choose several words you could use. Compare the different sections of the corpus to check which words are used in academic writing. For example, would it be better to choose *hitch* or *hindrance*?

7.2 Prepositions

A. Although prepositions (*at, on, for, with, to,* etc.) have core meanings, their use in academic writing is often idiomatic, which means writers have to learn the prepositions together with the verbs they complement and the nouns they qualify. This information can be found in any good dictionary or from a quick corpus search (7.1).

(1) Individuals can choose not to **agree with** government actions.

(2) The essay will begin with a brief historical **analysis of** plague outbreaks.

B. Some nouns and verbs are frequently followed by more than one preposition with different meanings. Some dictionaries may contain this information, but a search of COCA will often show the patterns more clearly. For example, in the academic section of COCA, the top prepositions after the noun *research* are *on* and *in,* followed far less often by *into, by,* and *with.* Each preposition adds a different type of meaning to the noun phrase.

(3) research **on** successful children [general topic]

(4) research **in** the field of substance abuse [field of study]

(5) recent research **into** bacteria in a California lake [very specific topic]

(6) research **by** the Centers for Disease Control and Prevention [agent of research]

(7) research **with** a small number of participants [study population]

C. Some words can be both nouns and verbs (for example, *research, influence, effect*), but they are not necessarily followed by the same prepositions. All three of these verbs are transitive and do not need a preposition with their object, but when used as a noun, they can be qualified by a prepositional phrase (1.2).

(8) The environment can **influence** a mental illness diagnosis.

(9) Managers **have a positive influence on** the hand hygiene compliance of their staff.

Exercise 5: Sentence Completion

Complete the sentences (from "Dentists could screen 20 million for disease," 2011) with an appropriate preposition. Use a dictionary or corpus to help you.

Dentists could play a crucial role ❶ _____ the front-line defense ❷ _____ disease, according ❸ _____ a study that finds nearly 20 million Americans visit a dentist every year, but not a general healthcare provider.

❹ _____ the study, published ❺ _____ the *American Journal* ❻ _____ *Public Health*, researchers examined the most recent available data ❼ _____ a nationally representative subsample ❽ _____ 31,262 adults and children who participated ❾ _____ the Department ❿ _____ Health & Human Services' annual National Health Interview Survey.

Physicians, nurses, nurse practitioners, and physician assistants were ⓫ _____ those categorized ⓬ _____ general healthcare providers ⓭ _____ the purposes ⓮ _____ the survey.

Exercise 6: Writing

These collocations are frequently used in academic writing, according to corpus research by Biber et al. (1999, pp. 1015–1018). Write sentences about a topic you are studying, using at least five of these phrases.

1. the start of _____.

2. the nature of _____.

3. the relationship between _____.

4. with the exception of _____.

5. shown in _____.

6. in contrast to _____.

7. similar to _____.

8. on the basis of _____.

9. the same way as _____.

10. an increase in _____.

7.3 Verb-Noun Collocations

A. Nouns may collocate with different words in writing than in speech. For instance, in COCA's conversational corpus, *do research* is the most common collocation, but in the academic section, *conduct research* is about twice as frequent as *do research*. A dictionary may provide this information, but you can also find it by searching COCA using the search term "[v*] research" (meaning, what verbs are used immediately before the word *research?*). You can also search wordandphrase.info. Other verbs found used with research include *address, support, review, base, extend, develop, provide,* and *participate.* It is, of course, important not to treat these as synonyms; they all have different meanings, as can be seen in Sentences 10 and 11.

> For more information and further practice with this shift in vocabulary from everyday words to Latinate words, see Unit 1 of *Academic Writing for Graduate Students,* 3rd edition.

(10) Data from Table 1 were used to **address** the four research questions and associated hypotheses.

(11) Self-report bias should be **addressed** in future research.

The verb *address* collocates not only with *research* but also (more frequently, it seems) with *research question.* Therefore, *address* is not a synonym for conducting research but refers to the questions that the research aims to answer.

B. Some verbs collocate with several nouns that share a common meaning. For instance, the verb *cause* is nearly always used with unpleasant collocations (Stubbs, 1995, p. 23). This means writers cannot write about causing a solution or a success. A quick search on wordandphrase.info confirms Stubbs's results. The top noun collocations are *problem, damage,* and *disease.* If you search COCA's academic section, some other top collocations appear neutral (*change* and *effect*), but further investigation still reveals negative connotations.

(12) Pollutants in water can cause **adverse health effects.**

(13) These human activities can cause **large-scale changes in marine ecosystems.**

Exercise 7: Sentence Completion

Use a corpus (COCA or wordandphrase.info) or dictionary to complete these sentences. The words in bold form part of the collocation. Compare your answers with a partner. Discuss whether different word choices change the meaning of the sentences.

1. Strong connections to school **exert** a powerful _____ in the lives of students.

2. The levels of chemicals that were found do not _____ safety **limits**.

3. Evidence-based arguments will _____ **flaws** in an opponent's reasoning.

4. International students are less reluctant to **seek** _____ with problems.

5. A criminal may _____ violent **actions** by claiming that he or she acted in self-defense.

6. New air bag test rules are intended to **minimize** the _____ of injury to small adults and children.

7. A foreign firm might be able to **maximize** _____ by selling its products in the United States at lower prices than in its home country.

8. We _____ a conceptual **framework** for thinking about species conservation.

Exercise 8: Writing

Choose five of the collocations from this unit and write sentences about your current research or field of study.

7.4 Noun-Adjective and Noun-Noun Collocations

A. Many adjectives collocate strongly with nouns. Adjectives can also be modified by an adverb that intensifies or qualifies its meaning, giving the pattern adverb + adjective + noun. Collocations using some of the adjectives from 5.7 (the most common adjectives in academic writing) include:

social + work, science, studies, skills, support, services

political + parties, science, power, system, economy

statistically, clinically, marginally + **significant** + difference(s), effect, role

important + role, part, factor, aspect, implications, component

B. Adjectives often collocate in highly idiomatic and unpredictable ways. Halliday (1966) observed that we drink *strong tea* but drive through *heavy rain*. Native speakers of English would probably never say *heavy tea* and *strong rain*. They do, however, speak about *strong winds,* so there is no relationship between *heavy* and weather words, for example. To search for an adjective collocation on COCA, use the code [j*] (any adjective) in front of a noun. You can also search <u>wordandphrase.info</u> for any noun and look at the adjective collocations (these are for the whole corpus, not just the academic section).

C. Noun + noun collocations are very common in academic writing. The first noun is called a **noun modifier** because it describes or classifies the head noun (1.2). Noun modifiers are usually singular unless the noun has a specific meaning in its plural form (*sales tax*). Noun/noun collocations have a very wide range of meanings, including the source, purpose, identity, content, and type of head noun (Biber et al., 1999, p. 590). Generally, a noun modifier is chosen over an adjective when an adjective form does not exist or has a different meaning (a *color photo* is not the same as a *colorful photo*).

(14) This paper looks at the problem of **college choice** in an environment with heterogeneous agents, competitive **admissions processes,** and **post-graduation wages** dependent on **college reputation.**

Exercise 9: Sentence Completion

Choose the best word to complete the sentences with the most idiomatic collocation. Use a dictionary or corpus to help.

1. The (fast / rapid) increase was perhaps partly due to better reporting of cases.

2. (Science / Scientific) theories can never provide a complete and definitive description of reality.

3. The current research was part of a (bigger / larger) study examining academic motivation.

4. The purpose is to promote mutual (understanding / communication) and friendship through photography.

5. High levels of (economic / financial) development tend to make people more tolerant and trusting.

6. People who interact with someone from another culture often experience (culture / cultural) shock.

Exercise 10: Paraphrasing

Simplify these noun phrases from an article in *Scientific American* (Moyer, 2010) by changing at least one prepositional phrase or relative clause into a noun modifier.

Example: access to broadband → broadband access

1. a policy about networks → _____

2. rules about open-access → _____

3. a student who scores C-minus → _____

4. the infrastructure of broadband → _____

5. a provider of service for the Internet → _____

6. Michael Powell, who was commissioner of the FCC → _____

7. a fee for transmission every month → _____

8. entrepreneurs of the Internet → _____

Exercise 11: Writing

Choose a page or two from an article or essay in your field of study. Highlight all the nouns with noun modifiers. Choose five noun modifier phrases and write your own sentences with them.

7.5 Skeletal Sentences

A. Many of the clause structures discussed in this text can be used as skeletal sentences. This term is used in *Academic Writing for Graduate Students* for the bare bones of a sentence that you can "flesh out" by adding your own content, such as *while the authors' position that . . . is attractive, there are a number of weaknesses in this concept* (Swales & Feak, 2012, p. 268). This section summarizes some of the major grammatical patterns that underlie these useful phrases using results from COCA searches. These searches can be replicated using the search string provided.

B. Many clauses start with the empty subject *it* and an adjective, followed either by a nonfinite *to* clause or a *that* noun clause (3.5). The searches for "it is [j*] that" and "it is [j*] to" provides these useful lists.

It is	clear	that . . .	It is	important	to . . .
	possible			difficult	
	(un)likely			necessary	
	true			hard	
	important			(im)possible	
	estimated			easy	
	imperative			interesting	
	evident			reasonable	
	obvious			essential	
	apparent			likely	

C. A related skeletal structure is *it* + passive reporting verb + *that* noun clause or *it* + modal verb + passive reporting verb + *that* noun clause. Searches for "it is [v*] that" and "it [vm*] be [v*] that" generate these phrases.

It is	estimated	that . . .	It should	be noted	that . . .
	assumed			be emphasized	
	expected			be remembered	
	hoped			be stressed	
	recommended		It could	be argued	
	believed			be said	
	suggested		It can	be argued	
	argued			be seen	
	said			be said	
	known		It must	be noted	

D. The present perfect tense collocates in academic writing with reporting verbs and *that* noun clauses (4.3). Frequent phrases used in academic writing result from the search for "[nn*] have [v*] that."

Studies			Researchers		
	have shown	that . . .		have found	that . . .
	have found			have suggested	
	have indicated			have argued	
	have demonstrated			have shown	
	have suggested			have noted	
	have reported			have reported	
	have revealed			have demonstrated	

Other nouns used in the corpus include *scholars, experts, authors, critics,* and *investigators.* Note that some verbs seem only to collocate with a human agent (*argue, note*), while most allow for either human or nonhuman agents.

E. There are some interesting skeletal frames involving relative clauses, especially clauses embedded in prepositional phrases (3.1). By conducting the search for "the [n*] [i*] which" three phrases most frequently: *the extent to which, the degree to which,* and *the way(s) in which,* but other common combinations include *the manner in which, the process by which, the context in which, the means by which, the conditions in which,* and *the frequency with which.*

(15) **The extent to which** these increased demands may have worsened the attrition rate is as yet unknown.

(16) Autonomy is broadly seen as the capacity of individuals to shape **the conditions under which** they live.

Exercise 12: Corpus Searching

Conduct these searches on COCA or MICUSP.

1. List skeletal phrases that begin with these phrases:

   a. may help _____

   b. may lead to _____

   c. may provide _____

   d. can be + passive voice _____

   e. will continue to _____

2. What grammatical structures are common after the prepositional phrase *based on*? Try searching for "based on the *", "based on [n*]", and "based on the [n*] that" to find the answers.

   _____

   _____

3. What are the most common types of complements that are used with *encourage* and *discourage*?

   _____

   _____

Exercise 13: Paragraph Writing

Write a paragraph on a topic you are currently studying in which every sentence contains at least one of the skeletal phrases discussed in this section.

Grammar in Your Discipline

A. Look through a piece of argumentative writing in your discipline. Examples would include editorials, letters to the editor, critiques, critical reviews, responses to articles, replies to those responses, and personal essays printed in trade publications or published as newspaper or magazine editorials or articles. Find examples of:

1. collocations

2. recurrent expressions

3. skeletal phrases

B. Look at the expressions and phrases you selected. Which patterns described in 7.3, 7.4, and 7.5 do they fit, or do they represent other patterns of collocations?

_____

_____

C. Share your findings with a small group of writers from other disciplines. Do you notice any similarities or differences? Which of the phrases could you use in your own writing?

_____

_____

D. Write an argumentative essay or position paper on a topic of current interest or controversy in your field of study, or write a letter to the editor or short article in response to a journal article or book you have recently read. Use a corpus and dictionary to help you write idiomatically using strong collocations.

Beyond the Sentence

This final unit looks beyond the sentence to the ways that grammar structures paragraphs and longer texts. At this point, the grammar of the clause becomes a tool for organizing writing because the textual function of grammar allows writers to organize words, clauses, and information in ways that are coherent (they fit the readers' expectations for this kind of text) and cohesive (clauses and ideas "stick" together in logical and acceptable ways).

Grammar Awareness: Textbook

Read two versions of the same text. Then complete the tasks on page 149.

Version 1: A great deal of planning needs to be done before making the decision to study here. The United States is a country with more than 4,000 colleges and universities, so one of the first steps involved in preparation is to decide which school you would like to attend. You may have a particular city or region in mind where you would like to study or a specific educational program in which you are interested. Your decisions should be made thoughtfully and carefully. Many people have wasted valuable time and money by selecting the wrong institution for their educational goals. It is important to do some productive research for yourself. Many college guides are available in book form and on the Internet that provide detailed descriptions about colleges, and some even rate the schools.

Version 2: Before making the decision to study here, a great deal of planning needs to be done. More than 4,000 colleges and universities are in the United States, so choose which school you would like to attend as the first step in your preparation. The choice of region is important, and you may be interested in a particular educational program. Thoughtfully and carefully is how you should make decisions. As for time and money, by selecting the wrong institution for their educational goals, many people have wasted them. Do some productive research: it is important for you. In book form and on the Internet, many college guides are available. Detailed descriptions and even ratings of the schools are provided by them.

148

1. Which version do you prefer? _____

2. Why do you think information flows better in one version than the other?

    _____

3. Where are the main (new) ideas in each clause? Does this help you answer Question 2?

    _____

    _____

    _____

8.1 Information Flow

A. In the grammar awareness task, most readers notice that the first version is much easier to read. Information flows quite smoothly from one idea and sentence to the next. However, in Version 2, it feels as if it is necessary to read each sentence backwards to understand the message. Sentences that start with new ideas are difficult to understand because readers only realize how those ideas fit the text at the end of the sentence. Although the paragraph is grammatically correct (there are no errors in word form, clause structure, etc.), the writer fails to use the textual resources of grammar to communicate effectively. (Version 1 is a published text from Shiraev & Boyd, 2008, p. 13; Version 2 is adapted from it.)

B. The normal organization of information in English clauses is old to new. This means that new and important information tends to appear later in the clause or sentence. Most sentences, therefore, should begin with old, familiar, or "given" information—something the reader can "recover" from context—and move toward information that is unfamiliar, unexpected, or "news" (Halliday & Matthiessen, 2004, p. 91).

C. Look again at Version 1 on page 148. If you highlight the important ideas—the guidelines for choosing a school—you should notice that they tend to appear late in the sentences. Furthermore, the paragraph flows smoothly because of the old-new information structure even without using any sentence connectors (*however, furthermore,* etc.).

Read another example. Why is it difficult to follow?

> ❶ All materials can be classified into three groups according to how readily they permit an electric current to flow. ❷ These are: conductors, insulators, and semiconductors. [. . .] ❸ All metals are conductors. [. . .] ❹ A material which does not easily release electrons is called an insulator.[1]

Circle the new information. Notice that two of the key new ideas are at the start of sentences (*all metals* in Sentence 3, and *a material which does not easily release electrons* in Sentence 4). The terms *conductor* and *insulator* are familiar since they were introduced in Sentence 2, but they appear in the "new" position in Sentences 3 and 4, which makes it harder for the reader to find and learn the new information.

---

[1] Example and analysis adapted from Martin, Matthiessen, & Painter, 1997, pp. 52 and 223.

D. Not all sentences have to start with old information—the first sentence of a paper or a new section, for example—and writers can sometimes start a sentence with new information for special effect, but they should use this technique carefully since it can be confusing.

Exercise 1: Language Analysis

Read the first two paragraphs of a recent scholarly book (Grenoble & Whaley, 2005) on language revitalization (*revitalization* means saving languages that are in danger of "dying" because too few people speak them). The sentences have been numbered 1-10. Finite, non-embedded clauses have been labeled $_i$ and $_{ii}$. Then complete the tasks.

❶ Over the past fifty years and with increasing frequency, innovative programs have appeared around the world with the aim of revitalizing languages that are at risk of disappearing due to declining numbers of native speakers. ❷ The nature of these initiatives varies as greatly as the languages that are their targets. ❸$_i$ In some instances, they are nearly national in scope, such as the efforts to preserve Irish, ❸$_{ii}$ yet in other instances they involve small communities or even a handful of motivated individuals. ❹$_i$ Many of these programs are connected to claims of territorial sovereignty, ❹$_{ii}$ though cultural sovereignty or a desire to maintain a unique ethnic identity is just as often the explicit goal. ❺$_i$ While in one context a revitalization effort may be centered around formal education, ❻$_{ii}$ in another it may be focused on creating environments in which the language can be used on a regular basis.

❼$_i$ Although tremendous variety characterizes the methods of and motives for reinvigorating languages, ❼$_{ii}$ revitalization, as a general phenomenon, is growing and has become an issue of global proportion. ❽$_i$ There are now hundreds of endangered languages, ❽$_{ii}$ and there are few regions of the world where one will not find at least nascent attempts at language revitalization. ❾ This comes as little surprise when considered in light of the confluence of several socio-historical factors. ❿ First, language death and moribundity (i.e., the cessation of children learning a language) are occurring at an exceptionally rapid rate.

1. Highlight or underline all the **new** information in the numbered clauses and sentences.

2. Use a different color or circle the **old** information. Note that not every clause has old information.

3. How do the authors create good information structure in these paragraphs?

_____

_____

8.2 Theme

A. The **theme** is defined as the first meaningful element in a clause. The theme is often the subject, but writers can make other parts of a clause the theme to improve the information structure or to focus the reader's attention. The theme is "the point of departure of the message," (Halliday & Mathiessen, 2004, p. 64), which is usually (but not always) old information. Themes are important because they tell the reader what the sentence is going to be about. Since writers often have quite a lot of control over which part of the element is the theme, this is a powerful resource for organizing a text. The themes in Sentences 1–3 are in bold.

(2) I analyze the data using the new method. [This is a statement about me.]

(3) **The data** were analyzed using the new method. [This is a statement about the data.]

(4) **The new method** was used to analyze the data. [This is a statement about the method.]

B. The theme can be changed to create better old-to-new information structure, to focus attention on one part of the clause, or to stress a contrast.

(5) The old method produced weak results. **However, the new method** produces stronger scores.

C. Notice that the theme includes any conjunctions (*and, because*, etc.), sentence connectors (*however, therefore*), and most adverbs (*usually, probably, evidently, unfortunately*) that are at the start of the clause. Importantly, some adverbs are most common in theme position (*however, therefore*), whereas others are almost never in the theme in academic writing (*also, too*).

(6) ❶ **We** commonly assume that children's development is in our hands. ❷ **Such a view** is reasonable enough, **and it** is shared by many psychologists. ❸ **Psychologists** use more scientific language, **but they** too assume **that parents, teachers, and others** structure the child's thoughts and behavior. ❹ **When they** see a child engaging in a new bit of behavior, **their first guess** is **that it** has been taught. ❺ **If, for example, a two-year-old girl** shows an intense interest in putting objects into place, **they** assume that someone taught her to do this, **for she** is a product of her social environment. ❻ **There** is, however, another tradition is psychology [. . .] **that** looks at development quite differently. ❼ **These writers**. . . .

In this paragraph, the themes move the text forward from what "we" commonly believe, to the psychologists' explanation of this view, and then to an example, and finally to an alternative theory. In Sentence 4, the entire dependent clause (*when they see a child engaging in a new bit of behavior*) can also be analyzed as the theme of the whole sentence, which forms a neat connection with the end of the previous sentence (*the child's thought and behavior*).

D. The theme is not always old information. In a typical clause, the theme is already known to the reader, but a writer can choose to put new information in the theme to disrupt the reader and add emphasis, or to highlight a contrast.

(7) **Tropical biomes** are characterized by a non-arid climate whose average temperatures remain above 18°C year-round. **Temperate biomes,** on the other hand, include a broader range of climates.

Exercise 2: Language Analysis

Underline the theme in each numbered clause in the following text, an excerpt from *On Being a Scientist* (Committee on Science, Engineering, and Public Policy, 1995). Then complete the tasks.

❶ Throughout the history of science, philosophers and scientists have sought to describe a single systematic procedure that can be used to generate scientific knowledge, ❷ but they have never been completely successful. ❸ The practice of science is too multifaceted and its practitioners are too diverse to be captured in a single overarching description. ❹ Researchers collect and analyze data, develop hypotheses, replicate and extend earlier work, communicate their results with others, review and critique the results of their peers, train and supervise associates and students, and otherwise engage in the life of the scientific community.

❺ Science is also far from a self-contained or self-sufficient enterprise. ❻ Technological developments critically influence science, as when a new device, such as a telescope, microscope, rocket, or computer, opens up whole new areas of inquiry. ❼ Societal forces also affect the directions of research, greatly complicating descriptions of scientific progress.

❽ Another factor that confounds analyses of the scientific process is the tangled relationship between individual knowledge and social knowledge in science. ❾ At the heart of the scientific experience is individual insight into the workings of nature. ❿ Many of the outstanding achievements in the history of science grew out of the struggles and successes of individual scientists who were seeking to make sense of the world.

⓫ At the same time, science is inherently a social enterprise—in sharp contrast to a popular stereotype of science as a lonely, isolated search for the truth. **⓬** With few exceptions, scientific research cannot be done without drawing on the work of others or collaborating with others. **⓭** It inevitably takes place within a broad social and historical context, which gives substance, direction, and ultimately meaning to the work of individual scientists.

1. Does the text mostly follow an old-to-new information pattern? Give two examples.

   _____

   _____

2. Look at the themes you underlined. Do you see any pattern of thematic development in the text?

   _____

   _____

3. The theme of Clause 8 is *another factor that confounds analyses of the scientific process.* Use your theme analysis to identify the three other factors.

   _____

   _____

   _____

4. What does *it* mean in Clause 13?

   _____

5. Find two examples of themes that contain new information. What is the effect of moving new information into this unexpected position?

   _____

   _____

8.3 Controlling the Theme

A. Writers use various grammatical resources to control the theme and move information into the old or new position. This section describes some of the most common, which should be evident in your readings and useful for writing.

B. An adverb, prepositional phrase, or dependent clause can be moved to the start of the sentence.

> (8) The locations of golf courses have changed since the sport's introduction to the United States in **the late nineteenth century. At that time,** golf was primarily a sport for the wealthy . . . .

The first sentence introduces the time frame (*the late 19ᵗʰ century*). Therefore, the linking prepositional phrase (*at that time*) is at the start of the second sentence as old information, and the new idea follows. The writer is possibly also setting up a contrast between then and now for a later sentence.

> (9) Similarly, Piaget tried to show that young children's conceptions of dreams are related to **egocentrism. As long as children are egocentric,** they fail to realize the extent to which . . . .

The dependent clause in the second sentence is old information that links to the new information of the first sentence.

C. Choosing passive voice moves the goal or recipient (one of the complements of the active voice verb) to the subject position, which is often the theme position.

> (10) This is Piaget's most famous experiment. In one version, the child **is shown two glasses, A1 and A2,** which **are filled to the same height.** The child **is asked if the two glasses contain the same amount of liquid** . . . .

The passive verbs (in bold) keep the new information (underlined) at the ends of the sentences, avoiding new participants that could interrupt the flow of information. The second sentence would be less clear if it were written as *The researcher then asks the child if* . . . .

> (11) You will have to obtain and submit letters of recommendation, often called letters of support. These letters **need to be written** by professors . . . .

The new information in Example 11 is that professors (not just anyone) have to write the letters, and the passive voice in the second sentence moves this information to the end of the sentence. Notice that the agent appears in the *by* phrase not because it is unimportant but because it is very important exactly who needs to write the letters.

D. The definite article *the* and pronouns *this* and *these* usually refer back to known information. In addition, writers can use nominalization (5.8) and general **summary nouns** (for example, *approach, aspect, challenge, criteria, difficulty, element, evidence, factor, fact, method, problem, reason, trend,* and *type*) to repackage the new information from a previous clause in a clear noun phrase at the start of the next one.

> (12) ❶ Yet it was against highfliers such as **these** [high-school students in England and Wales who choose to study mathematics] that the American students were in most cases being **compared.** ❷ Even when **the comparison** is not with foreign students but with other Americans, it is easy to draw misleading conclusions. ❸ **This** is particularly true with the Scholastic Assessment Test.[2]

Exercise 3: Sentence Writing

Read each sentence. Then write a second sentence that continues each idea using a synonym for the underlined general noun.

1. Many high school students have <u>problems</u> fitting in socially. These _____

   _____.

2. There has been a growing <u>trend</u> for graduate degrees to take longer. This _____

   _____.

3. There are three interesting <u>features</u> in the new design. These _____

   _____.

4. The first <u>stage</u> of the research was to collect data. In this _____

   _____.

---

[2] The first sentence is sometimes known as a "cleft" structure (Lock, 1995, p. 239). English allows writers to focus on almost any element of the clause in this way.

Exercise 4: Paragraph Revision

Read the beginning of an introduction to a research paper for an applied statistics course. Then complete the tasks.

❶ In neuroscience, the disorders of the central nervous system (CNS), which controls mechanical, physical, and biochemical functions of humans, have been one of the largest research areas. ❷ The research showed understanding the complex functionality of the human brain would be beneficial for degenerative CNS diseases such as Alzheimer's or Parkinson's. ❸ We used Functional Magnetic Resonance Imaging (fMRI), which is a noninvasive imaging technique for the human brain mapping field. ❹ Since the early 1990s, it has been a powerful tool in both research and clinical areas, helping further the understanding of brain functions.

1. Circle the old information in each sentence.

2. Underline the most important new information in each sentence.

3. Rewrite the paragraph so that it follows old-new information structure. Use some of the techniques described in this section.

8.4 Paragraph Patterns

A. There is no easy way to define a paragraph, but in most academic writing, a paragraph has several sentences that express one main idea or provide one step in the argument. Effective paragraphs can be described using the principles of theme and information flow introduced in this unit. The first three patterns on page 158 are based on the work of Frantisek Daneš described and confirmed by Robert Weissberg (1984), who found that "[scientific] research report writers regularly use topic development patterns based on the given/new contract in their published work" (p. 493). The fourth pattern is the one found in many writing textbooks.

B. In the **linking** pattern, the new information at the end of a sentence becomes the old information in the theme at the beginning of the next sentence, as shown in Figure 8.1. Weissberg (1984) found this to be the most common paragraph pattern in his sample.

Figure 8.1 A Typical Linking Pattern

Clause 1	Theme	New information
Clause 2	Theme (old)	New information
Clause 3	Theme (old)	New information

Based on Eggins, 2004, p. 324.

This pattern gives a paragraph a sense of gradual development, as in Figure 8.2 (Shiraev & Boyd, 2008, p. 13).

Figure 8.2 Example of Linking Pattern	
A great deal of planning	needs to be done before making the decision to study here. (NEW)
The United States (OLD)	is a country with more than 4,000 colleges and universities, so one of the first steps involved in preparation is to decide which school you would like to attend. (NEW)
You (OLD)	may have a . . . (NEW)

C. In the **repeated theme** pattern, several sentences or clauses share the same theme. The theme can be repeated using exactly the same word, a close synonym, or a pronoun.

(14) **The legislative branch of the U.S. government** is composed of the House of Representatives and the Senate. **The Senate and the House** make up what is referred to as the Congress. **The legislative branch** has always had "the power of the purse." **The control of the budget of the U.S. government** is a powerful check on the executive branch [the President and Vice President]. **The Senate consists** of 100 members. **Currently, the House** consists of 435 voting members. ᵢ **The House and the Senate** work on originating bills that set policy; ᵢᵢ **they** also decide how many of the government agencies should operate. (Shiraev & Boyd, 1998, p. 131)

Repeated theme paragraphs are useful for defining, explaining, or analyzing a complex concept. In Example 14 the writer breaks down the legislative branch of the government into its component parts and explains each one. Overuse of this pattern is not advisable because starting too many sentences with the same point (the same theme), does not allow the writing to move forward.

D. In the third pattern, one sentence contains a **super-theme,**[3] which is then broken into smaller parts in the themes of the following sentences (see Figure 8.3).

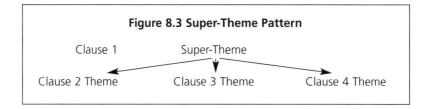

Figure 8.3 Super-Theme Pattern

In this paragraph from a popular book about linguistics, the super-theme is *brain*.

(15) ❶ When neuroscientists look directly at the **brain,** using a variety of techniques, they can actually see language in action in the left hemisphere. ❷ **The anatomy of the normal brain**—its bulges and creases—is slightly asymmetrical. ❸ **In some of the regions associated with language,** the differences are large enough to be seen with the naked eye. ❹ **Aphasics'**[4] **brains** almost always show lesions in the left hemisphere. (Pinker, 1994, p. 300)

Sentences 2–4 develop different aspects of brain research, becoming more specific (*brain* → *normal brain* → *language regions* → *aphasics' brains*) to support the main idea that language is primarily located in the left hemisphere. Notice that this pattern allows the ideas to develop within a defined topic, somewhat like a repeated theme. However, there is more development because the theme is explained through its component parts. The super-theme pattern is especially useful for describing complex systems and ideas, such as the brain in this example.

---

[3] Weissberg (1984) calls this a *hypertheme*, although this term is used differently in systemic functional linguistics (e.g., Hood, 2010), so this book adopts super-theme.

[4] Aphasia is neurological language disorder; an aphasic is a person with aphasia.

E. In the **theme preview** pattern, the first sentence of the paragraph introduces several elements in the new information (the end of the sentence). Each of these elements becomes the theme of one or more sentences in the paragraph. The first sentence, therefore, functions as a preview of the paragraph (sometimes called a **topic sentence**) (Figure 8.4).

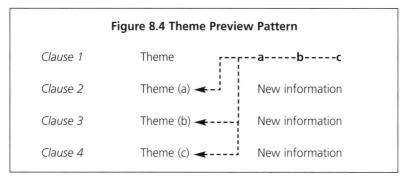

Based on Eggins, 2004, p. 325.

(16) The literature **offers four explanations for this puzzling phenomenon. The first explanation** is that good jobs come in bundles. Managers who know how to design one part of a job well are also likely to design other parts well, and are likely to work in organizations that treat employees well. **The second explanation** is that job satisfaction creates a halo effect. When employees are satisfied with their jobs, they are attitudinally biased to evaluate many aspects of their jobs favorably. **The third explanation** is common method bias. This explanation has been largely refuted, as several studies have shown that common method variance does not lead to the overprediction of self-reports. **The fourth explanation** is common source bias. Some scholars have argued that common source biases are responsible for inflated correlations between satisfaction and self-report variables. (MICUSP)

Theme preview is more useful for organizing long texts than single paragraphs. A literature review, for example, might begin with a preview of the main areas of literature under consideration, each of which is developed in several paragraphs (or a sub-section), using other patterns of development. When this method is used too often in an individual paragraph, the result can be repetitive.

F. These paragraph patterns can be extended over several paragraphs. It is also common to blend organizational patterns within the same paragraph, for instance, by defining and describing an idea with repeated theme structure (Sentences 1 and 2 in Example 17) and then developing it further with a linking pattern (Sentence 3).

(17) ❶ **Attribution theory** has been proposed to develop explanations of the ways in which we judge people differently, depending on what meaning we attribute to a given behavior. ❷ **Basically, the theory** suggests that when we observe an individual's behavior, we attempt to determine whether it was internally or externally caused. ❸ **That determination,** however, depends largely on three factors. (Robbins, 2003, p. 125, citations omitted)

In Weissberg's (1984) study, more than 20 percent of the paragraphs he analyzed combined two or more patterns in this way, leading him to conclude that there is "great flexibility" in paragraph structure in academic writing.

Exercise 5: Language Analysis

Read each passage. Underline the themes. Then identify the pattern. Discuss your choices.

1. Excerpt from an article in *Science Translational Medicine*, "The Road We Must Take" (Disis & Slattery, 2010)

But what evidence is there that the lone innovator is the source of most of our important discoveries?

Business researchers have attempted to address that question by studying patent data derived from the U.S. Patent and Trademarks Office. This data set is unique because it allows the study of teams versus individuals, is robust over a long period of time, and contains many data points across multiple types of inventions. Using an end point of how many times an individual patent is cited by future patents as a measure of its influence and success, investigators evaluated the success of lone versus team inventors. The number of citations for an individual invention has been shown to correlate with patent value and renewal rates.

Pattern: _____

2. From an article in a technology journal, "Gmail and Privacy Issues" (Freeman, 2006)

The anti-Gmail bill would forbid the technology from being used other than as a real-time analysis that would leave no trace or record. Specifically, the measure forbids an email provider from retaining personally identifiable information derived from the use of the technology. It also forbids human access to such information and forbids the transfer of such information to third parties. The bill also requires that when a consumer deletes an email, it must be physically, permanently deleted so no person or machine can ever retrieve it.

Pattern: _____

3. From an academic journal article, "The Cultural Psychology of Personality" (Markus & Kitayama, 1998)

The cultural shaping of personhood can be most obviously revealed and appreciated in Asian cultural contexts, where interdependent models of person are elaborated. Children are taught to appreciate the virtues of group life. Instead of celebrating individual accomplishments, special events recognize the accomplishments or growth of the whole group. Attention to and sympathy for others is among the primary goals of elementary education and it is crafted and fostered in many routine practices. Media and workplace practices also encourage being like others, being connected to others, and knowing not one's self, but others.

Pattern: _____

Exercise 6: Writing

1. Write one or two paragraphs on one prompt using linking (old-to-new information) organization. Think carefully about the theme of each sentence. Use the techniques in 8.3 to move information to the theme position.

   > For more information on how to create a research space in introductions, see Unit 8 of *Academic Writing for Graduate Students*, 3rd edition, and *Creating Contexts* (Feak & Swales, 2011).

   a. Choose an influential book or article you have read. Describe what the author wrote and why it is important in your field of study, work, or research.

   b. Choose an influential thinker, researcher, or practitioner from your field of work, study, or research. Describe what this person did to be considered important.

   c. Write an introduction for a paper you will or might write in your field. Use linking structure to explain the importance of the topic, what others have said about it, and how you are going to address it.

2. Write one or two paragraphs on one prompt using either the repeated theme or super-theme pattern. If you choose the repeated theme pattern, use different phrasing to make the writing interesting. If you use the super-theme pattern, think of words for its component parts or stages.

   a. Explain a complex concept from your field as if to a group of new students.

   b. Summarize the main idea of a book or article that you read recently.

   c. Describe a technique (for research, experimentation, analysis, or professional practice) that you are familiar with; explain what the technique is, where and when it is used, and why it is important to know.

Grammar in Your Discipline

A. Look at one or more examples of the type of writing that you will need to do. If you are taking graduate or undergraduate courses, search MICUSP or ask a professor or classmate. If you are preparing to write your thesis or dissertation, consult your university library for access to recent submissions in your field. Journal articles, grant proposals, and other professional genres are often available online or through libraries. Find examples of:

1. linking paragraph pattern

2. repeated theme paragraph pattern

3. super-theme paragraph pattern

4. preview paragraph pattern

B. Look again at the examples, and answer the questions.

1. Which patterns are most common? _____

2. Are particular patterns more common in different stages of the genre (e.g., Introduction, Methods, Results, Discussion)? _____

3. How are patterns mixed within and between paragraphs? _____

C. Share your findings with a small group of writers from other disciplines. Do you notice any similarities or differences?

D. Revise your current assignment. Pay particular attention to paragraph patterns and ways of controlling the theme. If it is helpful, write in the margin which patterns you are using, and ask a peer to review your writing and give you feedback on the cohesion.

Appendix: Verbs

Note: Verbs in the tables are listed from most frequent to less frequent.

Table A.1. Top 100 Verbs in the Present Simple Tense (Active Voice) in Academic Writing[1]				
be	give	reflect	tell	report
have	indicate	refer	believe	emphasize
do	involve	point	look	ask
say	continue	write	bring	examine
seem	go	explain	support	raise
provide	use	serve	happen	put
make	follow	lie	turn	leave
suggest	offer	reveal	claim	feel
appear	occur	consist	add	speak
become	exist	want	get	cause
require	describe	see	demonstrate	set
show	lead	increase	seek	move
remain	call	find	tend	cost
include	contain	help	stand	enable
mean	state	hold	produce	define
come	begin	note	play	relate
take	argue	know	affect	address
need	present	create	constitute	apply
allow	work	focus	illustrate	fail
represent	depend	imply	concern	run

Adapted from data in the Corpus of Contemporary American English (Davies, 2011).

---

[1] This is actually a list of the top 100 verbs found with a third-person singular *–s* ending in the academic section of the Corpus of Contemporary Academic English (COCA). The corpus is coded for word form (e.g., infinitive, *–s* ending, participle) rather than tense.

Table A.2. Top 100 Verbs in the Past Simple Tense (Active Voice) in Academic Writing (irregular past simple forms in parentheses)

be (was/were)	see (saw)	involve	choose (chose)	meet (met)
have (had)	ask	need	mean (meant)	increase
do (did)	seem	lead (led)	fail	represent
say (said)	want	seek (sought)	try (tried)	establish
find (found)	appear	start	grow (grew)	consider
become (became)	know (knew)	argue	examine	fall (fell)
make (made)	occur	work	allow	speak (spoke)
begin (began)	reveal	get (got)	serve	spend (spent)
come (came)	think (thought)	create	present	claim
report	continue	develop	learn	express
take (took)	note	bring (brought)	follow	conduct
include	remain	emerge	live	put (put)
use	provide	explain	complete	add
show	tell (told)	help	demonstrate	tend
write (wrote)	suggest	turn	participate	support
indicate	believe	conclude	observe	discover
go (went)	leave (left)	produce	agree	set (set)
receive	hold (held)	offer	perceive	experience
give (gave)	describe	call	play	publish
feel (felt)	state	decide	die	happen

Adapted from data in the Corpus of Contemporary American English (Davies, 2011).

Table A.3. Top 100 Verbs in Perfect Tenses in Academic Writing (Active Voice) (irregular participle forms in parentheses)				
be (been)	occur	note	seek (sought)	include
become (become)	provide	remain	attempt	die
have (had)	learn	try	indicate	get (got/gotten)+
make (made)	work	bring (brought)	point	decline
come (come)	suggest	produce	hear (heard)	suffer
show	focus	say (said)	know (known)	limit
take (taken)	create	call	pass	study
find (found)	grow (grown)	move	spend (spent)	put (put)
see (seen)	experience	play	complete	hold
do (done)	result	examine	turn	set (set)
lead (led)	write (written)	identify	live	read (read)
develop	fail	establish	allow	teach (taught)
receive	demonstrate	reach	adopt	rise (risen)
begin (begun)	prove (proven/proved)*	happen	undergo (undergone)	improve
change	lose (lost)	evolve	achieve	publish
increase	contribute	continue	describe	enter
use	serve	choose (chosen)	gain	acquire
give (given)	help	cause	observe	meet (met)
go (gone)	leave (left)	fall (fallen)	tend	decide
argue	emerge	report	appear	propose

* *proven* is slightly more common than *proved* in COCA, but the difference in frequency is minimal.
+ *gotten* is more than twice as frequent as *got* in COCA. In British English, only *got* is acceptable.

Adapted from data in the Corpus of Contemporary American English (Davies, 2011).

Table A.4. The Most Common Passive Verbs in Academic Writing

made	seen	found	considered
given	used	done	shown

Table A.5. Other Common Verbs Used in the Passive Voice in Academic Writing (in alphabetical order)

achieved	coupled (with)	extracted	linked (to/with)	reported
aligned (with)	deemed	flattened	located (at/in)	represented
applied	defined	formed	lost	required
approved	derived	given	measured	said
asked	described	grouped (with/by)	needed	situated
associated (with)	designed	held	noted	stored
attributed (to)	determined	identified	observed	studied
based (on)	discussed	illustrated	obtained	subjected (to)
born	distributed	inclined	performed	thought
brought	documented	intended	plotted	told
calculated	drawn	introduced	positioned	transferred
called	entitled (to)	involved	prepared	treated
carried	estimated	kept	presented	understood
chosen	examined	known	recognized	viewed
classified (as)	expected	labeled	regarded	
compared (to/with)	explained	left	related (to)	
composed (of)	expressed	limited (to)	replaced	

Based on Hinkel, 2004, pp. 166–167.

Glossary

*Words in **bold** are cross-referenced in this glossary. Parentheses indicate the section of the book where a more detailed description of the term can be found.*

action verb (1.5): a verb that describes what people and things do (e.g., *perform, study, design*). Action verbs can be **transitive**, **intransitive**, or **ditransitive**.

active voice (4.6): a clause in which the **agent** of the **main verb** is the **subject** of the clause (e.g., *we mixed the compounds*).

agent (1.5): the person or thing that does, causes, or is responsible for the **main verb**. The agent is the **subject** of an **active clause**. A **passive** sentence may not have an agent.

article (5.2): see **definite article** and **indefinite article**.

aspect (4.1): an element of the **verb tense** that tells the reader whether the verb should be seen as factual (simple), connected to a previous time (perfect), or ongoing (progressive).

auxiliary verb (1.1): a verb such as *has/have*, a form of *be*, or *do/does/did* that is used when the **main verb** is not the **finite verb**. See also **modal verb.**

bare infinitive (1.1): the infinitive form of a verb without *to* (e.g., *write, suggest, have*)

binary adjective (6.5): an adjective that is either true or not, such as *employed* or *stationary*. Binary adjectives cannot logically be modified with adverbs such as *very, somewhat, quite*, and they do not have **comparative** forms. However, some adjectives that could be considered binary by their meaning (*unique, pregnant*) are often made **gradable** in actual use.

boost (6.1): increase the strength of claims, for example, with certain **modal verbs** or adverbs or by word choices.

classifying adjective (5.7): an adjective that indicates the type of noun in the **head noun** position—for example, *a political party*. See also **noun modifier** and **describing adjective**.

clause (1.1): a group of words connected by a verb. Clauses can be divided into **independent** and **dependent** clauses. All independent clauses are **finite clauses**; dependent clauses may be **finite** or **non-finite clauses**.

collocation (7.1): the tendency of words to occur together (e.g., *heavy rain, strong tea*).

comma splice (2.7): see **run-on sentence**.

common noun (5.1): a noun that describes anything that does not need to be written with a capital letter (see also **proper noun**).

comparative (6.5): a form of adjective or adverb used to show the difference between two items (words, ideas, actions, states, etc.). The comparative form of **gradable** adjectives is *–er* or *more/less* + adjective. The comparative form of adverbs is *more/less* + adverb. Nouns can be compared using the **quantifiers** *much, many, few*, and *little*.

complement (1.1, 1.7): a word, phrase, or clause that comes after a verb and is controlled by the verb. Complements can take many forms, depending on the type and meaning of the verb. See also **direct object, indirect object, subject complement, finite clause, noun clause**, and **non-finite clause.**

complement clause (3.4): an embedded clause that completes the meaning of a noun or adjective (e.g., *the fact that . . .* or *it is important to . . .*).

complex sentence (2.2): a combination of one or more independent and dependent clauses.

compound sentence (2.2): see **equal clauses**.

conditional clause (6.4): see **real conditional** and **unreal conditional**.

conjunction (2.2): see **coordinating conjunction** and **subordinating conjunction**.

coordinating conjunction (2.2): a conjunction that can join two **independent clauses** as **equal clauses** (also called a **compound sentence**). The coordinating conjunctions are *for, and, nor, but, or, yet, and so* and can be remembered by the acronym FANBOYS.

corpus (7.1): a large collection of electronic texts that can be searched to discover patterns about particular uses of language (e.g., academic writing).

count noun (5.1): a noun that can be singular or plural. This means the noun has a shape or boundary, allowing you to *count* one or more. See also **non-count noun** and **double noun**.

definite article (5.5): *the*. The definite article is only used when both the reader and the writer can identify the specific reference of the **head noun**.

dependent clause (2.1): any clause that cannot be used as a complete sentence in academic writing. This includes all **non-finite clauses** and **subordinate clauses** (clauses with **subordinating conjunctions**, **relative clauses**, and **noun clauses**).

describing adjective (5.7): an adjective that describes the quality of the noun—for example, *an important question*. See also **classifying adjective**.

determiner (1.2, 5.2): a word that gives a reference to the **head noun** in a **noun phrase**: **indefinite**, **definite**, **generic**, **specific**, or **possessive**. The determiner helps the reader to determine what the head noun refers to: a category, any individual, a particular thing, or something belonging to someone.

direct object (1.5): the person or thing that is acted upon by the verb. In an **active** clause, the direct object is the **goal** of the verb. Direct objects are usually noun phrases, although they can be clauses with some verbs.

ditransitive verb (1.5): an **action verb** that requires two objects: an **indirect object** (functioning as the **recipient** in an **active** clause) and a **direct object** (the **goal**)—for example, *the university gave the team a grant*.

double noun (5.1): a noun that is usually **non-count** that has been made a **count noun**. In their countable meanings, double nouns can mean types, examples, or instances of the noun (e.g., *a wine* is a type of *wine*). In other cases, the count form has a boundary, which the non-count noun does not (e.g., *experience* is everything you have done until now; *an experience* is a particular event with a beginning and end).

elaborating clauses (2.5): **independent** or **dependent clauses** that describe or comment on the **main clause** without adding any particularly new information.

embedded clause (3.1): a clause that adds information about an element in another clause. Most embedded clauses are restrictive **relative clauses**, meaning they identify or define nouns. Sometimes, a **noun clause** can also be embedded with a noun that means *fact* or *idea*, in which case it acts as a **complement clause**, completing the meaning of the fact or idea.

enhancing clauses (2.5): **independent** or **dependent clauses** that add a time, place, manner, cause/effect, concession, or condition to the **main clause**.

equal clauses (also called **compound sentences**): two clauses with equal importance in a sentence, joined with the meaning of **expansion** with a **coordinating conjunction** or a semi-colon.

equative (6.6): a phrase or clause that describes two items (words, ideas, actions, states, etc.) as the same or similar. There are many resources for expressing equatives, including *as . . . as*, *the same as*, and *as many as.*

expansion (2.5): combining clauses by **elaborating, extending,** or **enhancing.**

experiential meaning (1.8): the event, action, or experience that the clause describes. Writers create experiential meaning through their choices of clause and sentence structure as well as vocabulary. All sections of this book, but especially Units 1–5, describe the resources for controlling experiential meaning. Experiential meaning is one of the three layers of meaning in **functional grammar** (see also **interpersonal meaning** and **textual meaning**).

extending clauses (2.5): independent or **dependent clauses** that add new information to the main clause.

finite clause (1.1): a **clause** with a **subject** that agrees with a **finite verb.** All **independent clauses** are finite; some **dependent clauses** are finite (e.g., **subordinate clauses** and full **relative clauses**).

finite verb (1.1): a verb that agrees with its **subject** (see **subject-verb agreement**) and can be changed to express different **verb tenses.**

fragment (2.7): a **dependent** or **non-finite clause** punctuated as a complete sentence. This is usually an error in formal writing, although proficient writers can use fragments to good effect.

functional grammar (Unit 1): a description of how language is used in context. Functional grammar is a way of understanding language not from the perspective of rules but rather from an analysis of how different choices affect the meaning of a sentence and a longer text. Functional grammar is interested in what language *does*, and functional linguists explain that language works by creating three layers of meaning simultaneously: **experiential meaning, interpersonal meaning,** and **textual meaning.**

future-in-the-past (4.4): a verb form describing an action or state that happened after another time in the past. The future-in-the-past is formed with *was/were going to*, or *would.*

generic reference (5.3): a **head noun** that means all of a particular category or group.

gerund (5.8): the *–ing* form of a verb; see non-finite verb.

goal (1.5): The element of a clause that is acted upon by the verb. In the **active voice,** the goal is the **direct object** (*the engineer fixed the network*), whereas in the **passive voice,** the goal is usually the **subject** (*the network was fixed by the engineer*).

gradable adjective (6.5): an adjective that can have a range of intensity—for example, by modifying it with an adverb such as *very, somewhat, quite.* Only gradable adjectives have **comparative** forms. See also **binary adjective.**

head noun (1.2): the main noun in a **noun phrase.** It is the head noun in the subject noun phrase that agrees with the **finite verb** (see **subject-verb agreement**).

hedge (6.1): reduce the strength of claims out of uncertainty or modesty, or show the source for your ideas—for example, through citation. Hedging resources include **modal verbs,** adverbs, **conditional clauses,** and many word choices.

indefinite article (5.4): *a* or *an* (no article is used for indefinite reference with a **non-count noun** or plural noun).

independent clause (2.1): a clause containing a **subject** and a **finite verb**. An independent clause can be a complete sentence in formal writing.

indirect object (1.5): the element of a clause with a **ditransitive** verb that receives the action of the verb. In an active clause, the indirect object is the **recipient** (*the professor sent the class an email*). Indirect objects can be noun phrases but are often prepositional phrases with many **action** and **reporting** verbs (*the teacher talked to the class*).

infinitive: see **non-finite verb**.

–*ing* verb: see **non-finite verb**.

interpersonal meaning (1.8): the relationship that a text builds between the writer and the reader. This level of meaning includes **hedging, boosting,** and evaluative language, as well as choices such as **personal pronouns** (first or third person?) and the use of questions (which directly address the reader). Unit 6 focuses on the resources for controlling interpersonal meaning. Interpersonal meaning is one of the three layers of meaning in **functional grammar** (see also **experiential meaning** and **textual meaning**).

intransitive (1.5): a verb that must have an **agent** (as the **subject**) but cannot take a **direct object**. Most intransitive verbs are usually followed by an adverb or prepositional phrase.

irregular noun (5.1): a noun with a plural form that is not formed by adding –*s* or –*es* (e.g., *children, criteria*).

linking (8.4): a pattern of paragraph organization in which the new information at the end of a sentence (or clause) becomes the old information at the start of the next.

linking verb (1.7): a verb that gives information about what something *is* or *is related to*. Describing linking verbs put the **agent** in a particular class or category (*She is a teacher*). Identifying verbs link the agent to its definition or to a statement about its identity, such as a name, example, role, symbol, or translation (*T is the response time*). The **complements** of linking verbs can be adjectives, **noun phrases**, prepositional phrases, and sometimes **clauses**.

main clause (2.1): in a sentence with more than one clause, the main clause is the **independent clause**. If there are two or more independent clauses, the first one is the main clause.

main verb (1.1): the verb in a **clause** that carries the main meaning, as distinct from an **auxiliary verb** or a **modal verb**.

metalanguage (Introduction): language used to talk about language—that is, the terminology used to describe grammar.

modal verb (3.2, 6.1): an **auxiliary verb** used to add **interpersonal meaning** to a **main verb**. The most common modal verbs in academic writing are *may, might, can, could, will, would,* and *should*. Modal verbs are often used for **hedging** and **boosting**.

modifier (1.2): a **determiner**, adjective, or **noun modifier** that appears before the **head noun** in a **noun phrase** and changes its meaning.

nominalization (5.8): changing a verb (or any other part of speech) into a noun phrase (e.g., *the reaction occurred quickly* → *it was a rapid reaction*).

non-count noun (5.1): a noun that does not have a plural form and cannot be used with **indefinite articles** because it has no shape or boundary and therefore exists as an uncountable concept. Many non-count nouns can become **countable**. These are called **double nouns.**

non-finite clause (1.1): a **clause** with a **non-finite verb** as its **main verb**. All non-finite clauses are **dependent clauses**. Some non-finite clauses are **reduced relative** (i.e., **embedded**) **clauses** or **non-restrictive relative clauses.**

non-finite verb (2.4, 3.5): a verb in the *to* infinitive (*to do*), bare infinitive (*do*), or *–ing* (*doing*) form that has no **subject** or a subject with which it does not agree in number. See **non-finite clause**.

non-restrictive relative clause (2.3): a type of **unequal clause** that **elaborates** on the meaning of something in the main clause with additional information, clarifications, descriptions, explanations, or comments. Non-restrictive clauses are always separated from the main clause with commas, unlike restrictive clauses, which are **embedded.**

noun clause (3.3): a dependent clause introduced with *that, if, whether,* or another *wh-* word. Noun clauses are usually the direct objects of **reporting verbs**. See also **subjunctive.**

noun modifier (7.4): a noun used as a **modifier** in front of a **head noun**. The modifier typically describes the type of head noun, for example—a *grammar* textbook.

noun phrase (1.2): a group of words that describe a main noun.

object (1.1): see **complement, direct object, indirect object.**

passive voice (4.6): a clause in which the **subject** is not the **agent** of the **main verb** (*The research was interrupted*).

past habitual (4.5): a verb form describing an action or state that was common or frequent in the past but is no longer so today. The past habitual is formed with *used to* or *would.*

possessive determiner (5.6): a word that specifies to whom the head noun belongs (*my, your, his, her, its, our, their*).

pronoun (1.3): a word that refers to a person or thing without naming it (*I, you, he, she, it, we, they*).

proper noun (5.1): a noun that is written with a capital letter because it is the name of a person, place, company, or trademark. All other nouns are **common nouns**.

qualifier (1.2): a prepositional phrase or **embedded clause** that appears after the **head noun** and explains or identifies it.

quantifier (5.6): an element of the **noun phrase** that specifies the quantity of the **head noun** (how much or how many), such as *many, a few, a number of.*

real conditional (6.4): a type of **enhancing clause** meaning that the main clause is true under certain conditions. In a real conditional, the conditions and the main clause are both factual (*they happened, are happening, or will/may happen*). See also **unreal conditional.**

recipient (1.5): the person or thing that benefits from the action of the verb. In the **active voice**, the recipient is usually an **indirect object** (*The experimenter gave the subjects clear directions*).

reduced relative clause (3.2): a relative clause can be reduced by omitting the **relative pronoun** and the verb *be* in some situations, or by changing the **finite verb** to an *–ing* **verb** in other situations.

referent (2.3): the noun, phrase, or clause that a relative pronoun replaces in a relative clause; in this definition, the referent of *that* is "noun, phrase, or clause."

relative clause (2.3, 3.1): a **dependent clause** in which a **relative pronoun** takes the place of one of a noun (the **subject**, **complement**, or object of a preposition). See **embedded clause** (for restrictive relative clauses) and **non-restrictive relative clauses**.

relative pronoun (2.3, 3.1): a **subordinator** used with a **relative clause**: *that, which, who, whose,* and *whom.* The relative pronoun can be omitted if it is the **direct object** of the verb in the relative clause, or in a **reduced relative clause**.

repeated theme (8.4): a pattern of paragraph organization in which the same word or idea is used as the **theme** of several sentences.

reporting verb (1.6, 6.6): a verb that reports the words, thoughts, or ideas of another person or source (e.g., *say, believe, claim*). A complete functional grammar would distinguish between verbal processes and mental processes.

restrictive relative clause (3.1): see **embedded clause**.

run-on sentence (2.7): two **independent clauses** joined with a comma and no **conjunction**. This is considered an error in formal writing.

sentence connector (2.2): an adverb or prepositional phrase used to show the logical relationship between sentences or **independent clauses**—for example, *however, therefore, for example.*

simple sentence (2.1): a sentence composed of one independent clause.

specific determiner (5.6): words that make the **head noun** specific *(this, that, these,* or *those)* when used in the **determiner** slot in the **noun phrase** by pointing to *this one* or *these ones* here, or *that one* or *those ones* over there. Specific determiners are often used with **summary nouns** or by themselves as pronouns.

subject (1.1): the element of a **finite clause** that agrees with the verb (see **subject-verb agreement**). In an **active** clause, the subject is the **agent** of the verb. Most **non-finite clauses** do not have subjects, but occasionally they may, for example, *I wanted the students to participate*, where *the students* can be considered the subject of the **infinitive** *to participate*.

subject-verb agreement (4.8): a feature of **finite clauses** where the verb is changed slightly depending on whether the **subject** is singular or plural. In the present simple tense, most verbs add an *–s* or *–es* with singular subjects. The verb *have* changes to *has*. The verb *be* has more forms: *I am, you/we/they are, he/she/it is* in the present simple tense, and *I/he/she/ it was* and *they/we were* in the past simple. When *be, have,* or *do* are used as **auxiliary verbs**, they agree with the subject. **Modal verbs** do not agree with their subjects.

subjunctive (3.5): a form of the verb used in **noun clauses** following verbs or adjectives with the meaning of recommendation, advice, or requirement (e.g., *recommend, insist, it is essential that*). The bare infinitive form of the verb (without *to* or third person *–s*) is used.

subordinate clause (3.4): a **dependent clause** that starts with any **subordinator**.

subordinating conjunction (2.2): a conjunction that can join a **dependent clause** to an **independent clause** in an **unequal** relationship, such as *because, if, although.*

subordinator (3.4): any word that introduces a subordinate clause, including **subordinating conjunctions**, **relative pronouns**, and **noun clause** subordinators *(that, if, whether,* and *wh-* **words**).

summary noun (8.3): a general noun with a broad meaning that is often used to create cohesion—for example, *difficulty, issue, feature*. Summary nouns are often used with **specific determiners** to create a link to a previous clause or sentence, a form of **textual meaning**.

superlative (6.5): a form of adjective or adverb used to show that an item (word, idea, action, state, etc.) is different from all others in some way. The superlative form of **gradable** adjectives is *–est* or *the most/least* + adjective. The superlative form of adverbs or nouns uses *the most/least*. Superlative noun phrases always require **definite articles**.

super-theme (8.4): a pattern of paragraph organization in which a main idea (the super-theme) is broken down into smaller parts or aspects in the **themes** of the following sentences.

tense (3.2): the meanings of time (past or present) and **aspect** that can be marked on a verb. Tenses in this book are described as time + aspect—for example, *present simple, past simple,* and *present perfect.*

textual meaning (1.8): the organization of the information and the message through an entire text (i.e. a paragraph, an essay, a paper, or a book). The textual function of language holds a text together and makes it coherent. This is done by choosing the **theme** of a clause and the position of new information. Unit 8 focuses on textual meaning. Textual meaning is one of the three layers of meaning in **functional grammar** (see also **experiential meaning** and **interpersonal meaning**).

theme (8.2): the first meaningful element in the clause. Typically, this is the **subject** plus any **sentence connectors** or **conjunctions** in front of it. The theme is "the point of departure of the message" (Halliday & Mathiessen, 2004, p. 64), which is usually (but not always) old information. Writers use the theme position to create certain patterns of organization in paragraphs and longer texts (**linking pattern, repeated theme, super-theme, theme preview**).

theme preview (8.4): a pattern of paragraph organization in which the **themes** of the paragraph are previewed in the first sentence (sometimes called a topic sentence).

time marker (4.2): an adverb or prepositional phrase that expresses the time period of the clause, such as *today, in 1997,* or *in three years.*

topic sentence (8.4): see **theme preview**.

transitive (1.5): a verb that requires an **agent** (**subject**) and **goal** (**direct object**) in the **active voice**. Transitive verbs can be used in the **passive voice** with the goal as the subject.

unequal clauses (a type of complex sentence) (2.2): an independent clause joined with a **dependent or subordinate** clause in a relationship of **expansion**. The dependent clause often starts with a **subordinating conjunction**.

unreal conditional (6.2): a type of **enhancing clause** that gives the conditions under which the **main clause** would happen, even though it is not possible now. Unreal conditionals can be hypothetical (what would happen now or in the future) or counterfactual (what would have happened in the past). See also **real conditional**.

voice: see **active voice, passive voice**.

wh- words (2.7): **subordinators** that can introduce **noun clauses** formed from question words: *who, where, when, why, whether, which* + noun, and *how* (+ *many / much*).

References

Biber, D., Johansson, S., Leech, G., Conrad, S., & Finegan, E. (1999). *Longman grammar of written and spoken English.* Harlow, U.K.: Pearson.

Brown, R. (1973). *A first language.* Cambridge, MA: Harvard University Press.

Carter-Thomas, S., & Rowley-Jolivet, E. (2008). *If-*conditionals in medical discourse: From theory to disciplinary practice. *Journal of English for Academic Purposes, 7,* 191–205.

Celce-Murcia, M., & Larsen-Freeman, D. (1999). *The grammar book: An ESL/EFL teacher's course* (2nd ed.). Boston: Heinle & Heinle.

Coxhead, A. (2000). The new academic word list. *TESOL Quarterly, 34,* 213–238.

Davies, M. (2011). *The corpus of contemporary American English: 425 million words, 1990–present.* Available at http://corpus.byu.edu/coca/

Eggins, S. (2004). *An introduction to systemic functional linguistics* (2nd ed.). New York: Continuum.

Feak, C. B., & Swales, J. M. (2009). *Telling a research story: Writing a literature review.* Ann Arbor: University of Michigan Press.

Feak, C. B., & Swales, J. M. (2011). *Creating contexts: Writing introductions across genres.* Ann Arbor: University of Michigan Press.

Folse, K. S. (2009). *Keys to teaching grammar to English language learners: A practical handbook.* Ann Arbor: University of Michigan Press.

Halliday, M. A. K. (1994). *An introduction to functional grammar* (2nd ed.). London: Edward Arnold.

Halliday, M. A. K. (1966). Lexis as a linguistic level. C.E. Bazell, J.C. Catford, M.A.K. Halliday, & R.H. Robins (Eds.), *In memory of J.R. Firth* (pp. 148–162). London: Longman.

Halliday, M. A. K., & Martin, J. R. (1993). *Writing science: Literacy and discursive power.* London: Taylor & Francis.

Halliday, M. A. K., & Matthiessen, C. M. I. M. (2004). *An introduction to functional grammar* (3rd ed.). London: Edward Arnold.

Hartnett, C. G. (1998). English nominalization paradoxes (ERIC No. ED426411). Paper presented at the Linguistic Association of the Southwest Conference, Tempe, AZ.

Hawes, T., & Thomas, S. (1997). Tense choices in citations. *Research in the Teaching of English, 3,* 393–414.

Hinkel, E. (2004). *Teaching academic ESL writing.* Mahwah, NJ: Lawrence Erlbaum.

Hood, S. (2010). *Appraising research: Evaluation in academic writing.* London: Palgrave Macmillan.

Hyland, K. (2000). *Disciplinary discourses: Social interactions in academic writing.* Harlow, U.K.: Pearson.

Lock, G. (1995). *Functional English grammar: An introduction for second language teachers.* New York: Cambridge University Press.

Martin, J. R., Matthiessen, C. M. I. M., & Painter, C. (1997). *Working with functional grammar.* London: Edward Arnold.

Stubbs, M. (1995). Collocations and cultural connotations of common words. *Linguistics and Education, 7*(4), 379–380.

Swales, J. M., & Feak, C. B. (2009). *Abstracts and the writing of abstracts.* Ann Arbor: University of Michigan Press.

Swales, J. M., & Freak, C. B.(2011). *Navigating academia: Writing supporting genres.* Ann Arbor: University of Michigan Press.

Swales, J. M., & Feak, C. B. (2012). *Academic writing for graduate students* (3ʳᵈ ed.). Ann Arbor: University of Michigan Press.

Warchał, K. (2010). Moulding interpersonal relations through conditional clauses: Consensus-building strategies in written academic discourse. *Journal of English for Academic Purposes, 9,* 140–150.

Weissberg, R. C. (1984). Given and new: Paragraph development models from scientific English. *TESOL Quarterly, 18,* 485–500.

References (Sample Texts)

A little to the left: Ahhhhhhhhhh. (2009). Retrieved from http://futurity.org/top-stories/a-little-to-the-left-ahhhhhhhhhh/

Bryson, B. (1996). *Made in America: An informal history of the English language in the United States.* New York: Harper Perennial.

Childhood obesity. (2010). In *Current issues: Macmillian social science library.* Retrieved from Gale Opposing Viewpoints In Context.

Chow, P. (2011). *What international students think about U.S. higher education: Attitudes and perceptions of prospective students in Africa, Asia, Europe, and Latin America.* Retrieved from www.iie.org/en/Research-and-Publications/Publications-and-Reports/IIE-Bookstore/What-International-Students-Think-About-US-Higher-Education.aspx

Cohen, J. (2009). A race against time to vaccinate against novel H1N1 virus. *Science, 325,* 1328–1329.

Committee on Science, Engineering, and Public Policy. (1995). *On being a scientist: Responsible conduct in research.* Washington, DC: National Academy Press. Retrieved from www.nap.edu/catalog.php?record_id=4917

Crain, W. (2000). *Theories of development: Concepts and applications* (4ᵗʰ ed.). Upper Saddle River, NJ: Prentice Hall.

Dentists could screen 20 million for disease. (2011). Retrieved from www.futurity.org/health-medicine/dentists-could-screen-20-million-for-disease/

Disis, M.L., & Slattery, J. T. (2010). The road we must take: Multidisciplinary team science. *Science Translational Medicine, 2*(22), 22.

English proficiency test gets F for stress. (2011). Retrieved from www.futurity.org/society-culture/english-proficiency-test-gets-f-for-stress/

Friedman, D. B., Rose, I. D., & Koskan, A. (2011). Pilot assessment of an experiential disaster communication curriculum. *Disaster Prevention and Management, 20,* 238–250.

Freeman, E. U. (2006). Gmail and privacy issues. *Information Systems Security, 15*(14), 2–6.

Gender gap persists among top test takers. (2010). Retrieved from www.futurity.org/society-culture/gender-gap-persists-among-top-test-takers/

Grenoble, L. A., & Whaley, L. J. (2005). *Saving languages.* New York: Cambridge University Press.

Hines, J. R. (1996). Altered states: taxes and the location of foreign direct investment in America. *American Economic Review, 86*, 1076–1094.

How the brain recalls what happened when. (2011). Retrieved from http://www.futurity.org/science-technology/how-brain-recalls-what-happened-when/

Hricko, M. (1998). Internet plagiarism: Strategies to deter academic misconduct. *Proceedings of the 1998 Mid-South Instructional Technology Conference.* Retrieved from http://frank.mtsu.edu/~itconf/proceed98/mhricko.html

Kelly Global Workforce Index. (2011). *Social media/networking: The evolving workforce.* Retrieved from http://media.marketwire.com/attachments/EZIR/562/8474_KGWI_SocialNetworking_report.pdf

Mamaghani, F. (2009). Impact of e-commerce on travel and tourism: An historical analysis. *International Journal of Management, 26*, 365–375.

Markus, H. R., & Kitayama, S. (1998). The cultural psychology of personality. *Journal of Cross-Cultural Psychology, 29*, 63–87.

Matsuda, P K. (1999). Composition students and ESL: A disciplinary division of labor. *College Composition and Communication, 50*, 699–721.

Michigan corpus of upper-level student papers. (2009). Ann Arbor: The Regents of the University of Michigan.

Microfinance success tied to macroeconomy. (2010). Retrieved from http://futurity.org/society-culture/microfinance-success-tied-to-macroeconomy/

Mild, um, speech pauses are persuasive. (2011). Retrieved from www.futurity.org/science-technology/mild-um-speech-pauses-are-persuasive/

Moyer, M. (2010). Bigger, better broadband. *Scientific American, 302*, 26.

National Institutes of Health. (2011a). How secondhand smoke affects the brain. Retrieved from www.nih.gov/researchmatters/may2011/05162011smoke.htm

National Institutes of Health (2011b). Weighing in on dietary fats: Some fats are healthier than others. *NIH News in Health.* Retrieved from newsinhealth.nih.gov/issue/Dec2011/Feature1

Online social networks. (2010). In *Current issues: Macmillian social science library.* Retrieved from Gale Opposing Viewpoints In Context.

Organic and locally grown foods. (2009) B. Wilmoth Lerner & K.L. Lerner (Eds.) *Environmental science in context, Vol. 2* (pp. 645–648). Detroit: Gale.

Pinker, S. (1994). *The language instinct.* London: Penguin.

Pollution haze mix may affect world's weather. (2009). Retrieved from www.futurity.org/earth-environment/pollution-haze-mix-may-affect-worlds-weather/

Robbins, S. P. (2003). *Organizational behavior* (10th ed.). Upper Saddle River, NJ: Prentice Hall.

Shiraev, E. B., & Boyd, G. L. (2008). *The accent of success* (2nd ed.). Ann Arbor: University of Michigan Press.

Star found hiding among Big Dipper friends. (2009). Retrieved from http://futurity.org/science-technology/star-found-hiding-among-big-dipper-friends/

Superstrong, superlight, and supersmall. (2010). Retrieved from http://futurity.org/science-technology/superstrong-superlight-and-supersmall/

Swim, J. K., Stern, P. C., Doherty, T. J., Clayton, S., Reser, J. P., Weber, E. U., and Howard, G. S. (2011) Psychology's contributions to understanding and addressing global climate change. *American Psychologist, 66,* 241–250.

'Text-therapy' may ease isolation. (2012). Retrieved from www.futurity.org/health_medicine/ 'text-therapy'-may.ease-isolation

To ignite economy, local beats global. (2011). Retrieved from www.futurity.org/society-culture/to-ignite-economy-local-beats-global/

United Nations Educational, Scientific, and Cultural Organization. (2009). *Global education digest, 2009: Comparing education statistics around the world.* Retrieved from www.uis.unesco.org/Library/Documents/ged09-en.pdf

Sources for Example Sentences/Texts

Full references can be found on pages 178–180. The numbers after each source are sentence/example numbers.

Unit 1
MICUSP: 1–6, 11–13, 17, 26
"Superstrong," 2010: 7, 8
Hines, 1996: 9
Invented: 14–16, 24–25, 27–29, 36–37
COCA: 18–23, 30–35
NIH, 2011: 38

Unit 2
"Online Social Networks," 2010: 2–11
MICUSP: 12, 18–19, 27–29, 43
COCA: 13–16, 20–26, 30–31, 44–45
"Childhood obesity," 2010: 32–34, 36–40

Unit 3
COCA: 1–2, 21–41, 52
MICUSP: 3–16, 42–48, 51

Unit 4
MICUSP: 1–14, 19–27, 29–32, 34–37,
    39–42, 46, 51, 58, 60–64
COCA: 15–18, 28, 33, 38, 47–50, 52–57,
    59, 65

Unit 5
Matsuda, 1999: 4, 10, 11
MICUSP: 5, 6, 8, 9, 12–15, 28–31
COCA: 7, 16–27, 32
Swim et al., 2011: 33

Unit 6
COCA: 1, 4–6, 8–21, 23–36,41–44, 46–50,
    56–60
MICUSP: 2, 3, 7,22, 37–40, 45, 52–55
"To Ignite Economy," 2011: 51

Unit 7
MICUSP:1, 2, 8, 9, 14
COCA: 3-7, 10–13, 15, 16

Unit 8
Martin, Matthiessen, & Painter, 1997: 1
Crain, 2000: 6, 9, 10
MICUSP: 7
COCA: 8
Shiraev & Boyd, 2008: 11, 13, 14
Bryson, 1996: 12
Pinker, 1995: 15
Eggins, 2004: 16 (adapted)
Robbins, 2003: 17